Social Hierarchies

Social Hierarchies

1450 to the present

ROLAND MOUSNIER
Professor at the Sorbonne, Paris

Translated from the French by Peter Evans

Edited by Margaret Clarke

SCHOCKEN BOOKS · NEW YORK

Contents

Social Hierarchies

Introduction

Some definitions and notes on method

Ever since the time of Hesiod and Plato men have, as they observed the behaviour and interactions of their contemporaries, created a mental picture of the society in which they lived as one of groups of people arranged in social layers or strata, one on top of the other, in a hierarchical order. These strata have usually been called 'classes', and it seems that classes, in the broadest sense of social hierarchy or stratification, exist or have existed in nine out of ten human societies. The relationships between these strata are an important factor in human history. Some commentators have indeed made them the dominant factor in social history as these relationships often constitute a form of social collaboration that is necessary to the life of any society. Theoreticians such as Suarez or Bellarmine found in this collaboration the ideal of the perfect society and considered that class divisions and struggles are by way of being a pathological phenomenon that, of necessity, calls for some kind of therapy. On the other hand, Karl Marx and the marxist thinkers after him, while not denying the existence of collaboration between classes, draw their inspiration from the philosophical theory of universal dialectics and see in class struggles the most striking manifestation of social life and, as it were, the very condition of the march of history. For politicians, sociologists and above all historians, problems of social stratification are fundamental.

Stratification in society derives from social differentiation and social evaluation. Differentiation in turn derives from the division of labour. The members of any society have different social functions to fulfil; be it the production of the basic material necessities of life, securing or providing services,

9

teaching, transport, domestic work, help and assistance etc.; governing or being governed; providing adequate defence measures (or attack), making an attempt to answer the perennial questions concerning man's ultimate objectives, his role in the universe, life hereafter and the spiritual world etc. In any society these functions should be and are fulfilled. Furthermore, as a society develops so these functions become more specialised although inevitably each individual does carry out more than one of them. The *Odyssey* shows Ulysses in the role of king or, in other words, simultaneously a warrior at the head of an army, high priest and judge as well as estate manager and carpenter etc., although the function of kingship dominates all these others. Even in societies in which the division of social labour is much more highly developed, the same principles obtain. Every man carries out several social functions of which the dominant one gives him his social designation.

This division of labour within society results in a form of social evaluation. Members of society evaluate each other by noticing how social functions differ in importance and to what extent there is disparity in performance within a given function. This type of evaluation operates on two levels. Firstly, it is a way in which a man judges what he can expect from another in his particular function because the other man is a means to his attaining his own ends. Secondly, it shows a man what another is worth in terms of the efficient functioning of the society in which they both find themselves, according to the conscious needs of that society. This type of evaluation is reflected in the *rank* each man is given on the social scale and expressed in the behaviour of individuals towards him (form of address, deference, influence, invitations, thanks, fees) and of society as a whole (rank, honour, decorations, salaries, pensions etc.) Looked at in this way, a system of social stratification is a machinery for meting out reward or punishment in order to ensure that individuals, groups or bodies carry out social functions that are either necessary to the existence of society or are judged as such.

Estimates of social worth are most commonly based on ill-defined, more or less vague, criteria which are frequently only implicit and of which people are hardly aware. They stem not from clear ideas and verified statements but from beliefs, impressions and opinions as often as not suggested by feelings and emotional leanings or attitudes, all of which are quite irrational and largely erroneous. This is the way in which value judgements are formed and established on the utility or otherwise of such and such a function and the ability of an individual, group or body to carry out this or that function. It is in this way that an important part of the basic structure of the whole of society is created.

Social functions are evaluated differently according to the fixed circumstances under which a given society is operating. For example, when there is a permanent danger of invasion, military functions are considered the most important and put at the top of the social hierarchy. Or again, if members of the society consider life after death more important than life on earth and value more highly their relationships with invisible beings, souls, demons, angels, gods and God himself, than worldly matters then the religious function of the priest is supreme. If, on the other hand, people consider life on earth, physical well-being and pleasure to be of cardinal importance then the production of material goods becomes central and engineers and technicians consider themselves as belonging to the top ranks of society. Any kind of social stratification depends on a number of value judgements which constitute the basic principle of the society in question. This basic principle can continue to dominate even when the circumstances that created it no longer prevail.

Social differentiation becomes more pronounced as the division of labour gets more elaborate. And, the more pronounced social differentiation gets the more complicated social stratification becomes, up to the point where a given class can consist of several strata, and one stratum several different social groups.

Theoretically, in a situation where there is a good division of social labour and a corresponding system of social stratification, social co-operation should be perfect and social equilibrium achieved without any class conflicts. In fact, every system of social stratification is in an unstable state of equilibrium within given limits. There are internal conflicts either to be overcome or arbitrated upon. The system requires, in fact, constant readjustment.

One reason for this is that members of society do not all make the same value judgements and social value judgements anyway are changeable. A certain number of people in society differ from the majority or depart from the value judgements that have been officially established by law or custom. These people feel a sense of injustice, maladjustment or oppression and feel the need to substitute one system of values for another. Accordingly they set themselves up in opposition to authority of different kinds and create conflict, disturbance and revolt with a view to overthrowing society itself.

Another reason for the relative instability of social systems is that even if people are in agreement on the fundamental social values, those who carry out a social function may believe that their particular function does not enjoy its rightful place in the hierarchy. They have a sense of illogicality and injustice which again leads to conflict, disturbance and revolt. The difference between this category of dissenter and the one described above lies not in the outward manifestations of their discontent but in their overall objective, namely to reorganise parts of a system that in the broadest terms is acceptable.

Lastly, the third reason for social readjustment is that even if members of a social organism are in agreement on social values and their own rank within the social strata, tensions and clashes will periodically recur quite simply because the more conscientious people are the more convinced they are of the importance of their main social function. So they become keener to discharge it perfectly and thereby tend to lay claim to excessive recognition for their function within the overall structure. If the rest of society were to let teachers and students have their way, these two groups in their striving for perfection would make half the population into teachers and commit half the national budget to education alone. The Department of Transport and Highways would weave a spider's web of motorways over the whole country, empty the coffers of the State and municipal organisations, disfigure beauty spots and destroy ancient monuments etc. etc. Everyone would absorb an excessive share of the nation's total resources for his or her particular social function. Every individual tends to forget that any society is made up of a collection of necessary social functions each of which should only be developed in accordance with the proper functioning of the whole, however short of the ideal this degree of development may be in absolute terms. The common weal can require a number of social functions not to reach their highest conceivable level because if they did they would necessarily drain off too large a share of the total resources available. However, the best exponents of the social functions strive to perfect them as a result of their interest in the common weal, their wish to emulate others, or through corporate or individual ambition, and so create a situation of rivalry between themselves and other people carrying out other functions. The result is tension, clashes, conflict, strikes, disturbances and revolts which are struggles between social functions, professions or corporate organisations and have no connection with class struggles or struggles between different ranks, 'orders', or 'estates'.

Each of the social functions is evaluated according to the amount of knowledge required to carry it out as well as the amount of responsibility involved, and as often as not these two factors are evaluated by general opinion. In this case, so far as knowledge is concerned, it is a question of the mental agility and shrewdness that are indispensable in carrying out a given social function. The more general and systematic this knowledge is the more value is placed on it. This conclusion accords with that of Voltaire and d'Alembert who were very surprised that the great innovators in the realm of algebra were famous while the inventors of the saw, the plane or the fusee chain and escape mechanism of the watch remained unknown.

Responsibility means the authority and ability needed to direct the activities of a certain number of members of society, to organise their work and direct their efforts subject to social sanctions in the event of failure of the person in charge. The greater the responsibility, the higher the value placed on the particular function.

In different societies the same social need may be satisfied by different social functions and different social needs satisfied by a single social function. So the name given to a function only describes imperfectly its nature and the social need to which it is suited. If one needs confirmation of this one has only to consider the different kinds of activity covered by the term 'king', from the negro tribe to the Athens of antiquity, or Saint Louis, Louis XIV, and Louis-Philippe the First, King of the French. Two writers, both with the same social function of 'novelist' can differ by being in the USSR a government employee, in the US a freelance creative artist. Names of social functions in the professions, for example, are misleading. The same name can cover different activities according to the type of society involved.

Individuals are evaluated and classified in the social hierarchy or stratification first of all by virtue of their main social function, what they do for the common good, and this usually corresponds to a profession or job. Yet other criteria come into play in this evaluation and, according to the society in question, some of these criteria constitute conditions under which a given profession or job is carried on. One might take into account race or at least birth, parentage, or lineage as is done in societies with a hereditary aristocracy. Or one might consider connections such as marital alliances. Sometimes the consideration is religious purity, the degree of purity within a given religion as is the case in India, or at least the nature of the professed religious beliefs when there is a hierarchy of religions as in the United States not long ago, or again the hierarchy of beliefs such as was found in the Third Republic in France when freemasonry then socialism were at the top of the scale. One might take property into account, however small this might be, or wealth, although the latter is often the direct result of social function, rank and the means of maintaining the life style appropriate to it. One might consider secondary, community activities that require only a limited amount of time or a minor degree of involvement such as the functions of president, secretary or committee member of a club, a learned society, a charitable organisation, a church council or a secret society. One can even take personal qualities into account.

These criteria are grouped together into different categories to give different scales of social stratification which are linked together and usually act in combination to establish rank. There are often discrepancies in that one person may be placed high on one of these scales and low on another. We must distinguish between the four kinds of scales of social stratification.

Firstly there is *legal stratification*, as expressed by law, custom and jurisprudence. This does not exist in every stratified society. Many societies with highly developed systems of stratification are without the legal one, for example nineteenth-century France, with a few exceptions. Furthermore, legal stratification never conveys the overall system of social stratification. It can also be different from the real social structure.

The second scale, and probably the most important, is *social status*, or in other words differences of social esteem, position, rank, honour and prestige among individuals and social groups (such as families, organisations, colleges, communities) and mutual recognition of these differences in a given society. Social status shows itself initially in all the various forms of connections; marriage ties (the most important of all connections), trade unions, political parties, clubs, circles and societies of various kinds, and academies. It is seen in social symbols and myths, etiquette, life style, manners, education, forms of entertainment, and in family backgrounds. It is seen in one's profession, and in moral sensibility, feelings and emotions. A person's mentality also enters into the issue, his way of seeing, judging and reasoning; his beliefs, opinions, values, wishes, the things that satisfy or dissatisfy him, as do his attitudes or his tendency to react in a certain way to outside stimuli or to behave in a particular way. Social status is seen in the roles people play, these being based on the prescribed model behaviour for everyone with the same status. In short, status is seen in a person's behaviour from morning till night, every day of his life. For each of these aspects, we must distinguish between the conscious value attached to them by a man's contemporaries and the real value reflected in the behaviour in question.

The third scale of stratification is the *economic hierarchy*, all too often confused with the social hierarchy itself. Here we must look firstly at the nature of the resources available, whether wages or salary, private or investment income etc. The kind of resources available are far more important than their size because it corresponds in part to the role played by the individual in the production of material goods. Next, we must categorise the different kinds of wealth or capital; landed property whose position in law (freeholds, manor, fief, copy-hold for example) must be distinguished from its farming unit (direct exploitation, shared cropping and tenant farming). Then there are industrial, commercial and craft enterprises with their plant, tools, their stocks of raw material and manufactured goods; then public services; unearned income of various kinds; letters of credit, bills of exchange, promissory notes, bank deposits. There is the hoarding of treasures in the shape of precious metals, jewellery, silver plate, coins, furniture, works of art, libraries. There is the total amount of wealth, capital, income or profits and the general state of a given fortune in the light of what is known of its past history. Lastly there are the differences in prestige that accrue in the eyes of one's contemporaries to different categories of possessions and different types of wealth.

The fourth scale is that of *power*. By this we mean all those ways by which one man can bend the will of others towards making them act as he chooses them to act. This is the way governments operate as do administrators, magistrates and various kinds of representatives or officials. Likewise there are economic pressures such as those exerted by a creditor on his debtors, or a manager on his employees or a wholesaler on a retailer etc. The way in which preachers, orators, pamphleteers, journalists, pressmen, radio and television men all influence public opinion is a form of power. Furthermore, we should not overlook individual charisma, that quality of personal influence possessed by certain men who command our attention and support. And so on and so forth.

Lastly, the fifth scale of stratification is the *ideological* one. In any society there are groups of ideas that hang together though they are not held in equal esteem. To declare allegiance to such and such a group of ideas is to bring either praise or blame on oneself, securing either the highest governmental or administrative functions or excluding

2

oneself from them, opening or closing doors to certain careers and certain levels of social status.

It is necessary to draw up these various scales and examine their connections, correlations and deviations, in order to see clearly the stratification of a given society and thereby assign a place within it to an individual or social group. Many politicians and sociologists have omitted to do this in their attempts to define the concept of social class. Sometimes they have done this by laying stress on economic stratification, sometimes on political or professional stratification at the same time forgetting that social stratification is the result of these three factors combined, together with a few others. Thus, Aristotle, Plato, Menenius Agrippa, Sallust, Voltaire, Raynal, Guizot, Enfantin, Considérant, Godwin, E. Bernstein *et al.*, understood by the term 'social class' the strata of poor and rich, taking as the only kind of social stratification the economic one, even at times only that of wealth and income, or level of consumption. Helvetius, Saint-Simon, Blondel and others distinguished the dominant, aristocratic, exploiting and privileged classes from the subordinate, submissive and exploited classes. Or, in other words, they took political stratification to mean social class. Turgot, A. Bauer to a certain extent, K. Bücher again only in part, G. Schmoller, V. W. Taussig etc. took jobs and professions as the main basis for social classes. Karl Marx did not leave behind him a coherent theory of social class. His thinking on the subject has to be pieced together from numerous scattered fragments. For Marx a social class was a group of people playing the same role in the production process. Class was basically determined by the role played in the organisation of labour and its performance. Income, life style, education, the distribution of wealth and prestige, all these did nothing more than give an indication of an individual's position. They are symbols, not the underlying reality.

All these theories appear to be the result of an inadequate

analysis of social realities, of an incomplete view of these realities. A more penetrating analysis of society shows that, in order to define a social stratum, one must combine several groups of factors that are linked by the interplay of action and reaction, the chief factors being social status, economic situation and power.

The term 'social class' has had from the socialist writers of the nineteenth century onwards a particular significance. In this book, the term is retained for certain types of societies. But when discussing social stratification in general, the term 'social stratum' which is free from any specialised meaning, is used instead of 'social class'.

Therefore, if we think of the men who go to make up a given society as being hierarchically arranged in a scale of layers or levels, a social stratum is a layer that includes groups which sometimes are bodies or morally inclined people with a medium for expressing a common will.

Social strata stem from the division of social labour. They exist through the division of social labour, independently of all ownership of the means of production. A social stratum is characterised by the amount of social labour assumed by its members, be this in government, administration, defence or conquest, religion, science, production etc., by the form this social labour takes and by the degree to which it has at its command the social labour of another stratum or other strata.

The prime requirement is therefore co-operation between strata. The division of social labour implies co-operation. In the beginning there was co-operation. However, members of a given stratum differ from members of other strata in and through their social function, in and through the share of social labour they undertake. This social function, this share in the division of social labour constitutes their whole life, their *raison d'être*, their way of living, their means of maintaining their life and improving it. The more important this share is, the more important they are and the better their life is. The desire to wield power needs to be satisfied just as much as, indeed more so than, material needs. Therefore, with the creation of social strata, rivalry between strata occurs and, while co-operative relationships are of fundamental importance there springs from this rivalry quite another group of social relationships which are antagonistic.

The division of social labour originates in a series of value judgements, more or less explicit and inspired by the desire for power, on the necessity, usefulness, importance, rank, honour, greatness of different social functions. These value judgements differ according to the society, and therefore every system of social stratification is different from every other system, although they can be classified according to types, whence we can draw hierarchical concepts. In general, value judgements may be hierarchical, arranged according to the power, real or imagined in a given society, attributed by this society to such and such a social function. From this, according to the society, results the pre-eminence of the priest or the warrior, of the Elder, the industrialist, or the scientist etc.

The concept of the social stratum is a universal one that designates a type, a collection of given qualities, considered apart from the whole gamut of social attributes. It includes general concepts of social strata. The social stratum is a 'family' which includes different 'species': order, caste and class.[1]

Note to the Introduction

1. See Roland Mousnier: 'Le concept de classe sociale et l'histoire', *Revue d'Histoire économique et sociale*, XLVII, 1970, pp. 449–59.

Part One

Three Main Types of Social Stratification

This section does not study every system of social stratification that has existed since the middle of the fifteenth century, but only a few types that have come about in a certain number of societies and which have played an important part in history throughout this period. Firstly we shall look at social stratification by 'order' and 'estate', then stratification by caste, and finally stratification by social class proper.

Chapter One

Social stratification by order

Social stratification by 'order', subdivided into 'estates' (in German *Stände*, in French *Etats*) is extremely common. It consists of a hierarchy of degrees ('estates' or 'conditions') each one distinct from the other and organised not according to the wealth of their members nor their consumption capacity, nor yet by their role in the process of production of material goods, but according to the esteem, honour and rank that society attributes to social functions that can have no connection at all with the production of material goods. 'Orders are permanent ranks and are closely bound up with the lives of those who are honoured by them unless they are lost through abuse', according to a Frenchman, Loiseau, a jurist living in a typical order-based society in the seventeenth century. In India, at the beginning of the Vedic period, there were in the Rig-Veda three orders or 'colours' (Varna); the Brahmin, or poet and priest, the Kshattriya or warrior and chief and the Vaisya, or common man. In feudal France up to the middle of the fifteenth century as well as in the France of fealties that followed this period, social prestige, honour and rank were ascribed to the military profession and the fitness for leadership and protection that derived from it. In the China of the Ming and Ts'ing dynasties, from 1368 to the Revolution in 1912 social prestige, honour and rank went to the graduate scholar whose vocation lay in public office.

Thus, all societies of orders are based on consensus, a tacit agreement that derives from the particular set of circumstances in which society finds itself at a given time. This consensus determines the most important social function, namely

23

the one that establishes one social group at the top of the social hierarchy. Thereafter the established principle of classification continues to exist, and can do so, for hundreds or thousands of years, independently of the circumstances that gave rise to it. A number of factors combine to perpetuate this principle. There is the general interest that everyone has in maintaining the social order together with fear of the dangers created by a major upheaval. Or there is force of habit which makes it difficult to conceive of another social order. Then there are the gradually evolving links between the existing social order and a whole intellectual system which lends it rational justification. And lastly, there is the tendency of the dominant group in society constantly to engineer the same circumstances which orginally gave rise to a given type of social stratification like, for example, wars in the case of feudal society. Social groups arrange themselves according to their proximity or distance from the social function and life style of the dominant group as well as according to the nature of the services they provide for this group. In a military society, authority and organisational ability are essential social functions. Thus, the social groups nearest to the dominant military groups are those whose function involves authority, organisation and the general and systematic knowledge that makes these possible, namely magistrates, then scholars and important merchants. The military needs the man of law to transform the act of force into law, to organise social relations in a judicial manner, and thus ensure social equilibrium. They need merchants to acquire precious metals, rare and exotic produce and the basic materials of warfare. At the bottom of the social scale are those whose social function and way of life are the furthest removed from those of the dominant group, in the case of a military society, wage-earning manual workers. Peasants, artisans, clerks, bearers of court orders (bailiffs), and attorneys, undoubtedly provide indispensable services but they are looked down upon as common, wretched and unworthy. There are numerous rungs in the ladder of social hierarchy and it would not be correct to reduce it to a straight split between those who are exempt from manual work and those who are bound to it.

Every social group has imposed upon it a consensus of opinion as to its social status, that is to say, its rank, honour, rights, duties, privileges, obligations, social symbols, dress, food, coats of arms, way of life, upbringing, its way of spending money, entertainments, social functions, the profession its members should or should not have, the behaviour its members should display in their relationships with members of other groups in various situations in life and the behaviour they can expect in return, the people they should mix with and treat as friends and equals, and those they should simply coexist with and with whom they should only mix in the course of their social function or through necessity etc. Social status as a rule determines how rich or comfortable each person becomes because it enables one to receive a greater or lesser share of society's income in the form of wages, salaries, bonuses, allowances, pensions, annuities, services, exemption from taxes or other general expenses.

Within every social stratum there are organisations, societies or elected bodies forming action groups, each with its own social status resulting from a consensus of opinion as well as its customary or legal status. Groups with a common style of existence strengthen lineages which are linked together by marriage and form interrelationships which tend to be something of a closed circle.

An order can comprise several social strata or 'estates' or correspond to only one stratum. Generally speaking the social strata comprise several groups, each having a common style of existence. In each of the 'estates' that goes to make up an order we see a tendency towards endogamy which is compensated for by female exogamy. This is, however, only a tendency and not the rule.

In each of the 'estates' that goes to make up an order we also see a tendency towards the principle of heredity. We can in this context perhaps talk of a caste tendency when we find a concern for hereditary purity of blood.

Social mobility is possible for a given family or dynasty. On average three generations are needed to change orders, sometimes to change 'estates'. Social mobility is controlled and restricted by society. The newcomer must have his quality acknowledged by his new 'estates', tacitly, through the behaviour of its members towards him as well as by the state which officially gives notice of this change of status.

The majority of these features are only imposed upon the situation by social pressures, by a consensus of opinion. In general, a very restricted number of them receive legal sanction from custom and law.

A society of orders can change completely if the social esteem in which the various social functions are held happens to change. If in a military society the greatest social esteem is given to magistrates or men of law generally, then the whole social hierarchy changes and as a result is rearranged according to the pre-eminence of jurists who become the nobility or the most distinguished men in the nobility. Despite this change, the society in question remains a society of orders if social classification continues to derive from a consensus of opinion on the pre-eminence of a particular social rank and not from religious purity or the part played in the means of production of material goods.

Stratification by order seems to me to be a fundamental kind of stratification, the one most frequently found and one that is brought about naturally as soon as the division of social labour reveals social differentiation. It is the type of stratification that can re-establish itself spontaneously during any long drawn-out social upheaval and the one that all societies come back to after deviating from it. And it is the type of stratification that tends to predominate in the second half of the twentieth century in which we live.

Chapter Two

Social stratification by caste

An order-based society can evolve into a society of castes. This happened in India where, during the Vedic period, the society of orders was further complicated by a fourth and inferior 'colour', that of the 'Blacks' or Dasa, the Sudra, the conquered ones, destined to serve the Arya, the invaders, or 'Whites' who made up the three orders of Brahmins (or priests), Kshattriyas or Rajanyas (the warriors and nobles) and Vaisyas (or common folk, farmers and merchants). Towards the end of the Vedic period, around 600 B.C., the Brahmin order had every appearance of a caste. Bit by bit the caste system spread through every sector of the population and diversified. In this instance, castes originated in the impact created by two races.

The social groups we call castes form a hierarchy not by virtue of the wealth of their members or their consumption capacity, nor yet by virtue of the part they play in the production of material goods, but rather as a result of their religious purity or impurity. Relationships between people or groups of people are based on mental, religious and ritualistic representations. Society is fragmented into groups living apart from each other, each in its own independent little world. Society is divided according to the inherited degree of religious purity. Strict rules indicate to each group whom its members may approach or touch, from whom they may obtain food or drink and what kind of food and drink this shall be, whom they must avoid and who for them are untouchables. A morbid fear of contamination keeps each group apart from all the others. Respect for religious purity is what strengthens the social hierarchy.

In India, at the top of this hierarchy are the castes of the Brahmins, or priests, whose lives are devoted to religious worship and teaching. Second in rank come the Kshattriya castes whose members are soldiers or politicians and administrators. These castes competed with those of the Brahmins during the period 600 B.C. to 300 A.D., but were vanquished by them and led an increasingly secluded existence even to the point where they are considered to have been destroyed after 1100 A.D. The third rank in the hierarchy is made up of the Vaisya castes, the farmers and merchants who after the year 1100 A.D. are often confused with the Sudras. Last of all are the Sudra castes who devote their lives to the service of the other castes. Among these are the unclean and untouchables. The four categories were subdivided into an ever-increasing number of castes each forming part of a hierarchy within each category. At the end of the eighteenth century there were in existence probably around two hundred hierarchically arranged castes subdivided into about two thousand sub-castes hierarchically arranged within the main castes.

In caste-based societies, an individual's status does not depend on his abilities, valour or good fortune, but solely on his belonging to such and such a sub-caste, which determines his station in society, the behaviour of others towards him and the behaviour they can expect of him towards them. However, belonging to a given sub-caste is purely a matter of birth. Religious purity derives from purity of blood so belonging to a caste is a racial matter. The individual belongs to the sub-caste into which he is born, to which his parents belong. He necessarily spends his whole life in the same sub-caste and his children in turn belong to it. The individual cannot, whatever his deeds, achievements or successes move up into a higher sub-caste. There is no individual social mobility. A sub-caste can in its entirety elevate itself by one degree if it follows a calling to lead a more religiously pure kind of life and if it succeeds in getting the other sub-castes to accept this change. Should an individual succumb to an appalling uncleanness he can be banished from his sub-caste whereupon he is forbidden to enter any other. He becomes casteless, an outlaw, a reject.

Endogamy prevails in sub-castes. An individual must marry within it and suffers the penalty of expulsion for failing to do so. A Konkanastha Brahmin must marry a Konkanastha; a Karhada Brahmin a Karhada. It is not unknown for women to practise exogamy but this involves the risk that the children can be forced to form a new sub-caste.

As a rule the sub-caste has its profession or occupation. Brahmins are priests, Chambahrs are shoemakers. In fact, a limited number of professions or occupations are accessible to a given sub-caste so one specialised hereditary group cooperates with all the other specialised groups by bartering for goods and services. General well-being should ensue if each caste carries out its work correctly and without fail. No sub-caste has the right to change its occupation or profession but if it overproliferates or becomes unproductive it can carry on another, less honourable one. There is practically no market for goods and labour. Fixing prices remains a feeble business. Sub-castes have to work together in symbiosis and harmony, never changing functions or encroaching on the functions of their fellow-men. A sub-caste's activity is not simply a situation or job but a religious way of life. Profits or income differences are not what induce an individual to carry on a given activity because the producer of goods does not measure the value of his services by means of what he could earn in producing other goods. Sub-castes have no occasion to operate in the industries that earn the biggest profits. The social basis of production is collaboration, reciprocity and settlement, harmony rather than grasping opportunities in a competitive situation. This principle becomes modified by necessity so that if a caste traditionally has one occupation several others are allowed besides, and, in practical terms, certain occupations such as farming, being a soldier, and commerce are open to a number of castes. Some Brahmins are soldiers, farmers and traders.

Every sub-caste has its own way of life only a part of which is its occupation or profession. A sub-caste has its privileges, its outward signs, its ceremonies, its forms of worship and its religion which is part and parcel of Brahminism. This way of life is imposed on the individual who can practically only eat and drink with members of his own sub-castes. The sub-caste's council or Panchayat, made up of members of the sub-caste sees to it that its rules of conduct are adhered to and sanctions any breach of them. Eating, drinking or having any kind of contact with a member of another sub-caste whom it is forbidden to frequent; maintaining a concubine from another sub-caste; breaking with one's sub-caste's customs regarding marriage and other ceremonies; insulting a Brahmin; killing a cow or any other sacred animal; filching another man's customers; raising or lowering prices; ignoring the special business practices of one's sub-caste; non-payment of debts; refusing to honour a promise of marriage; being guilty of brawling; indulging in fornication or adultery with a married woman etc; all these are sins against the religious purity of the sub-caste and are punishable by its council.

The caste system is not a mechanical one. It is a mental picture that individuals have within different groups of what the behaviour of their group towards others should be as well as how others should behave towards them. Although the overall system is accepted this does not prevent frequent rivalry between sub-castes in order that one may move up to a higher rank in the hierarchy. Sub-castes can rise higher either by assuming an occupation that is considered purer and having this change agreed to by the other sub-castes, or by usurping social symbols of superiority. Thus, among the Marathas, the potters maintain the custom of conducting the bridal procession on horseback, while the carpenters are opposed to this practice. The Lingayats lead their processions through the street while the coppersmiths object to this. Members of rival sub-castes come to blows, create disturbances and revolts in order to snatch from other sub-castes the symbols of higher social esteem. At Vaykam in Travancore, unclean sub-castes agitate to gain free access to certain streets that are reserved for purer sub-castes.

Winning a greater degree of social esteem and a higher place in the social hierarchy is certainly a matter of self-esteem, pride and personal dignity but it is also a source of economic advantage. In Bengal the cost of renting land varies in inverse proportion to the rank of the tenant's sub-caste. The Brahmin as such enjoys tax reliefs and customs duty exemptions as well as gifts from all members of society. The king is the Brahmins' protector and protection of the Brahmins is one of the state's highest functions. In fact, in this highly segmented society liaison between social groups is ensured by the priest who is necessary for carrying out religious services.

To complete this picture of the concept of caste, we might quote the Englishman who wrote that the Madras census of 1911 suggested 'a division of the population of England into families of Norman origin, priests in holy orders, noblemen, positivists, iron merchants, vegetarians, communists and Scotsmen'. In other words, each caste can correspond to a race, a religious order, an aristocracy, a philosophical and political doctrine, a form of commerce, a diet, a nation and many other kinds of social groupings. This is the social value of a system that allows the most heterogeneous and antagonistic social groups to live alongside each other.

Chapter Three

Social stratification by class

Social classes are a category of social strata that exist in societies with a market economy where the production of material goods and the creation of wealth are judged the most important social functions and where capitalist production relationships dominate. Classes are, therefore, social strata distinguished one from another by their share in the production of material goods, the kind of labour they provide; ownership or lack of ownership of the means of production, the mode of ownership and exploitation (whether work is entrusted to others or done by the owner alone, whether freely or in a situation of dependence), their market situation (whether a wholesale supplier able to dominate the market or a retail shopkeeper dependent both on the wholesaler and his customers; whether making an indirect commercial contribution by way of land or finance etc. or a direct commercial contribution through one's labour), the greater or lesser degree of control over prices, having the labour of others at one's disposal or, on the contrary, being obliged to put one's labour force at the disposal of someone else (the labourer or farm worker), the independence of a business (property divided in small portions) or the opposite situation where the enterprise is in a state of dependence (craftsmen working for industries), and legally free social mobility subject only to the laws imposed by the economy and to social value judgements. Classes are also distinguishable one from another by differences in life style, interests, ways of thinking and ideologies. A social class may be said to be 'perfect' if, in addition to the above aspects, one also finds a common consciousness and unity of action. In the nineteenth century typical class-based societies existed in

Europe, particularly north-west Europe around the North Sea and the English Channel, and in North America.

Karl Marx did not formulate a complete theory of social classes. He was tackling the question in Chapter 52 in Volume Three of *Capital*, when his death interrupted the work. If one takes this chapter alongside different passages in his other work, we see that in Marx's view, what created a social class was 'at first sight the same income or sources of income'. However, because income is a function of different kinds of property, classes are characterised in the last analysis by the ownership or non-ownership of the capitalist means of production. In his *Critique of Political Economy* in 1859, Marx wrote: 'I examine the structure of the bourgeois economy in the following order: Capital, Property, Wage-earning Labour; State, external Trade and World Market. Under the first three headings, I study the economic conditions of the three great classes into which modern bourgeois society can be sub-divided.' Thus, the three main social classes are the capitalists whose basic income derives from profits; the property-owners whose income comes from interest and rents and finally the wage-earners. To Marx, in fact, surplus value, that is the increase in value created by the labour over and above the value of this labour in terms of goods, breaks down into profit for the entrepreneur (be he industrialist, trader or banker), interest and ground rent, while the value of the labour in terms of goods is wages.

On the other hand, Marx distinguishes between two kinds of capital, the active and that without any function. The latter is the capital of capitalist money lenders which gains interest or dividend without taking an active part in directing the economic process, or, in other words, the capital of the different kinds of rentiers. Lastly, while analysing profits, Marx discovered that a fraction of these were not derived from surplus value but were by way of remuneration that a boss paid himself for his own work. Marx called this a 'supervisory (or management) salary' and it was thus no longer capitalist profit. For Marx, moreover, a class-based society would only exist when class ties went beyond a local framework and became national in character, in a national community, equipped with a political organisation.

However, although Marx with his adherence to economic analysis, gave us a good description of the economic structure of social classes in the capitalist framework of his time, he was unable to go far enough in social analysis as such. In fact, ever since Marx's time a class had been coming into being which was drawing a management salary and, economically speaking, was part of the wage-earning class, being, like its members, in opposition to idle and even active capital, but which on the other hand was socially distinct from the wage earners and formed an embryonic technocracy. Further, Marx's three classes were socially differentiated internally into a great many separate classes. Lastly, Marx, in formulating his theory, described an ideal form of capitalism which has never in fact existed because he had eliminated from it all the non-capitalist elements existing in capitalist society. The peasants, artisans and small traders living within the system modified in economic terms the autonomous trends towards expansion or contraction and profoundly changed class relationships, social and political life.

Max Weber stressed the idea of market restrictions. For Weber social class is defined in terms of the opportunities its members have in the market. A class situation is a market situation. Classes are differentiated according to the possibilities their members have in the market. Four main social classes can be distinguished. Firstly there is the property owning class with goods to sell but who are not forced to sell them. These people are in a position to transfer property from its use as 'wealth' or as a consumption asset to its being used as 'capital' or a production asset, with a view to making a profit; in other words a class of property owners capable of becoming entrepreneurs.

Below them in the social hierarchy are the non-productive property-owning rentiers. Below these again, the class of producers who are forced to dispose of their produce at any price in order to make a living.

Lastly, at the bottom of the social scale, come those who have only physical strength and manual skill to offer on the labour market.

A given class situation can bring about similar reactions and lead to mass action. If the cause and effect relationship in a class situation is clearly apparent and if the disparity of individual opportunities is keenly felt as a result either of a particular allocation of property or of the structure of the economic order, then that class can structure itself into an organised entity with a management, staff and course of action calculated to bring about a rational adjustment of the interests involved.

T. H. Marshall, who was greatly influenced by the example of the U.S.A., believed that social classes were groups of people with the same position within the economic system. A class system was for him a social structure in which social stratification is controlled by one's position in the economic system. In the capitalist U.S.A. of his time, the social hierarchy corresponded to the power structure within the business firm, from the head of the concern to the casual worker. Social groups, broadly speaking, corresponded in society as a whole to the functional hierarchy within firms. To the theoretician Marshall, the typical class-based society might have existed in the U.S. during the last quarter of the nineteenth century. This was the golden age of independent entrepreneurs, the 'old middle class', who only constituted a third of the productive section of the population but they represented the ideal type of American citizen in a competitive, capitalist economy. Every citizen aspired to the position they occupied, and it was believed that any citizen 'who had the guts for it' could indeed reach a similar goal. It was an idealised picture of a world in which talent and enterprise could triumph, a world built on a belief in basic social equality. It was thought the only differences between citizens, equal at the outset, were those by which success was measured; the amount of wealth acquired, economic inequality. This was the purest kind of class-based society.

The three theories analysed above are linked predominantly to the economic structures of the class-based society. In addition to the features these theories bring out, we should also add some social aspects. Class-structured societies are societies containing talent and ability. Below the big businessmen but high in the social strata, come groups of people whose intellectual contribution are a necessary and established feature and who receive their remuneration from different kinds of payment, be these salaries or fees. As well as management personnel and top technical staff within firms (engineers), this group comprises lawyers, barristers, notaries, attorneys, magistrates, civil servants, most of whom, in any case are themselves men of property, rentiers or even capitalists.

Class-based societies are open societies in which individuals are free and equal by law. The law recognises only individuals not social groups. Social classes are a fact of life but they have no legal existence. A social class has no governing body provided for by law, no official regulations, no legal sanctions for any violation of behaviour which is tacitly agreed on as the norm by its members. A social class is the purest form of a group, a collection of individuals with the same attitudes, same role, same instincts and same basic ideas.

In principle, social mobility is at its most highly developed in this type of structure. The individual climbs the social ladder as and when he becomes more powerful in the production process, acquires more wealth and transforms this more and more into capital. The only form of heredity in social terms is the inheritance of property, the only official social group is the 'nuclear family' of father, mother and their children. In principle, too, there is no endogamy or if there is, it is no more than a tendency stemming from a concern to find an equal marriage partner and a counter-balance to one's fortune or captial.

In fact, by inheriting property the sons of bourgeois capitalists have the best career opportunities and the most efficient means of preserving or bettering themselves as regards education, influence and capital resources. Lineage is maintained, far more than theory might suggest, reinforced by marriage ties and assisting in the conquest of social rank by its customary mutual aid. Social mobility is restricted by the need to acquire the life style of the higher levels of society to which the individual aspires, and this is something that is not always possible to a man who has recently acquired a fortune. It can take two or three generations. Lastly, the bourgeoisie in Europe were for a long time legally privileged as the law forbade for much of the nineteenth century trades unions, trade guilds and strikes. It favoured the bosses in court hearings of labour disputes and kept a special watch on the working man, However, in considering these facts, we are obviously out of the realm of pure theory and we are no longer considering an ideal version of a class-based society.

Chapter Four

Intermediate types of social stratification

Pure forms of society are very rare. The historian most often comes across intermediate types which do not belong to any one classification but show the characteristics of two types of society merging gradually one into the other. He also frequently encounters societies which certainly belong to one type because this type predominates, but embody, as it were encysted within them, social features belonging to other types of social stratification. Let us examine some examples of these two aspects.

England, from the end of the fifteenth century to the twentieth century, illustrates the slow transition from an order-based to a class-based society. The social group occupying the highest strata in the social hierarchy are 'gentlemen'. Now these never constituted an 'estate'. Since the sixteenth century, 'gentlemen' have had no legal and political status, no rights to which they can lay claim before the courts, no titles, no special functions. An individual is a 'gentleman' through a consensus of opinion, through being accepted by other 'gentlemen' who all agree on this assessment.

The term 'gentleman' embraces the aristocracy, the gentry, some members of the bourgeoisie, certain landowners, certain members of the liberal professions, a few chosen members of the business world. 'Gentlemen' and 'ladies' nonetheless constitute a very real social group. To belong to it, one needs essentially to have the education, manners, bearing, gait and countenance of a 'gentleman' together with his culture and way of life, in which the total absence of any manual work is a key element. One's birth, family background, and fortune (or at least having sufficient money to lead the life of a 'gentleman'), all play an important part. The symbol of belonging to this group is the right to avenge an insult by a sword fight, the right to duel. One only fights in this way against one's social equals.

Conversely, in the U.S.A. we find social groups whose existence probably indicates the change from a class-based society to an order-based society in the making, which is of course not yet legally recognised. In twentieth-century America, the proportion of independent entrepreneurs is declining. There are fewer and fewer chances of gaining economic independence. The economy is changing from 'atomic' capitalism to 'molecular' capitalism, from the firm owned by the entrepreneur using his own capital and that of his family and a few friends to the big joint-stock company, to combines, cartels and holding companies. Capital is more and more controlled by the power and policies of big capitalists on the one hand and the power and policies of organised, labour unions on the other. It is under these conditions that a 'new middle class' is developing, drawn mostly from the minor liberal professions and wage-earning employees destined to remain in the middle strata of the capitalist hierarchy without a hope of reaching the highest levels. Thus, there arises within this class a fresh preoccupation with social status, a greater importance attached to anything which signifies social rank, the outward signs and symbols of social position, such as correctness of manners, good pronunciation, academic achievement, having old school friends. This kind of society tends to be a closed one. In fact 'estates' seem to be in the process of forming.

Max Weber believed that rapid progress in technology, production and profit caused class situations to occur and, conversely, that long spells of economic stability and more so of economic recession create order situations. Within one type of social stratification staying the same for a long time in a given geographical location, it is possible that, according to differing combinations of circumstances, at different periods and in different places, kinds of stratification might appear which bring to mind other types of stratification. It is possible that class structures might appear within a predominantly order-based system or that order structures might appear within a predominantly class-based system. This is what the ethnologists W. Lloyd Warner and Paul S. Lunt seem to confirm with their work on *Yankee City* (Newburyport, in New England) carried out around 1933. In this small town of approximately 10,000 inhabitants the economy of which suffered from a protracted recession, the researchers found a type of social stratification that suggested an order-based society, in the heart of the U.S. where, at that time, a class structure still predominated. In Newburyport, the highest social stratum was the 'upper crust' boasting uninterrupted lines of descent from the eighteenth or nineteenth century. All these families formed a single, closely bound group that kept all the others at arm's length. Its members used the terminology of kinship among themselves, calling each other 'cousins'. 'She is my cousin, not in actual fact, but because my mother and father were brought up with her.'

This 'upper crust' was endogamous. There were family ties among all its members. Before marrying they compared genealogies and rejected upstarts. Marriage with a first cousin was a frequent occurence. 'My children are descended from the first immigrant of the T . . . . . family, in sixteen different ways, nine on their mother's side, seven on mine'. Many girls remained spinsters rather than marry below their station.

This 'upper crust' had special forms of behaviour, distinctive manners and way of life. Family meals were a veritable ritual. There were rituals for every act in life, even when putting away toys. Heirlooms had a ritual value, as a symbol, linking the living with the dead as well as drawing the members of a household closer together. The family home was a veritable shrine to one's ancestors, a symbol of the lineage. Money was of secondary importance and the 'upper crust' included people who were not comfortably off: 'You can have little money, but it's the way you use it that counts."

Members of other social strata were conscious of the existence of the 'upper crust'. To the question 'Why does "the richest man in our town" not belong to the upper crust?', those who themselves did not belong replied, 'He and his family do not behave well, they don't do what one should do', they do not mix with the people they should; 'they do not belong to the right families'. In short 'the richest man' did not observe the behaviour and life style proper to members of the 'upper crust' and so this social stratum remained closed to him despite his wealth. However there is no doubt that in the long run, wealth, by allowing one to lead their way of life should allow access to the 'upper crust'. Moreover, wealth made for marriage with certain girls from the 'upper crust'. But wealth by itself was not what counted in getting an individual accepted as a member of the 'upper crust'; it needed two generations of a life-style.

The researchers even found in the 'upper crust' a number of myths explaining and justifying the social order. The 'upper crust' was said to be descended from sea captains settled in the region; the middle stratum was descended from the ships masters, second-class petty officers and leading seamen and the lowest strata from the ordinary sailors.

Thus, we see here many of the features of an order-based society in the midst of a society which overall is structured into classes. Conversely, it is not impossible to find that within an order-based society circumstances have combined to produce what looks like class situations. In Segovia during the first third of the sixteenth century merchants had perhaps become the leading social group through their role as capitalist businessmen, that is to say, as a social class.

It is not even impossible to find that, within societies stratified into castes, circumstances combine to produce what look like class situations. According to G. S. Ghurye,[1] in 1670 in southern India, artisan castes contended with the Brahmins for social supremacy. If the facts be averred, these artisans could not have been acting in the name of religious purity. They could only have been moved to compete by some vague feeling that activities that produced material goods were superior to religious activities. Could this movement have been such as to have some connection with the development of Indian trade within India and with Europe? With the growth of capitalist businesses calling on the labour of these artisans?

Note to Chapter Four

1. G. S. Ghurye, *Caste, Class and Occupation*, Bombay University, Department of Sociology, 1961, Chapter 1, p. 6.

Part Two

Towards a Classification of Societies of Orders

Chapter Five

The typology of societies of orders

1. Some types of societies of orders

Societies based on orders or 'estates' are certainly the most numerous of all societies. The term can therefore cover societies that differ greatly one from the other so, in this welter of varieties, it is necessary to distinguish different types. A society of orders is based on the social esteem, rank and honour granted by a consensus of opinion to such and such a social function which may have no connection at all with the production of material goods. The basic organisational principle governing these societies lies in this consensus. Thus there are as many types of societies of orders as there are basic organisational principles governing them.

We can now therefore draw up a provisional list of different types to be studied in greater detail. One can easily distinguish first of all those orders based on the social pre-eminence given to the military profession, especially to the profession inherited from time immemorial such as feudal France, in the France of fealties in the sixteenth and again in the seventeenth century, perhaps in China during the Ming dynasty, in the fifty years following the national revolt and the expulsion of the Yuans Mongol.

Then we have societies of orders based on the lofty rank accorded the magistrature and to the learning that gives rise to this vocation, as was the case in China during the Ming and Ts'ing, and in seventeenth and eighteenth century France where the principle of social superiority of the magistrature was in conflict with the principle of social superiority of the sword and, in fact, perhaps carried the day.

After these would come the 'liturgical'[1] societies based on

49

the principle of social pre-eminence being granted to those dedicated, preferably hereditarily, to the service of the state as for example in the Muscovite state in the sixteenth and seventeenth centuries.

We should also distinguish between the different kinds of theocratic orders based on the social superiority of the ecclesiastic, such as in the Roman state in the sixteenth, seventeenth and eighteenth centuries (and, doubtless, earlier than that), in the Tibetan state and even the Genevan state at the time of Calvin and Théodore de Bèze, although it will no doubt be argued that a pastor is not an ecclesiastic. The theocratic orders differ from caste-based societies in that their sacerdotal nature is not passed on by virtue of birth or blood line, as with the Brahmins.

There are then the 'philosophical' orders in which eminence of social position springs from adherence to an overall vision of the universe and humanity such as Roman Catholicism, the philosophy of the Enlightenment, Marxism, Nazism, Fascism, and the commitment of the individual to getting this 'philosophy', this *Weltanschauung* to prevail. Societies of this type are, among others, France at the time of the Second League (1585–1598), the French Republic of 1793, Fascist Italy, Hitler's Germany and Soviet Russia.

Lastly, there is a type of technocratic society of orders in which the scientists and technicians enjoy the highest rank and which Saint-Simon and Auguste Comte conceived of. This type of society seems to be coming into being in several parts of the world.

2. *Two phases of societies of orders*

The examples of the League in France, of 1793, of Italian Fascists, Nazis, and Soviets all show how every 'philosophical' society of orders goes through to successive stages. The first phase is when the society is created, when a new social strati-

fication emerges based predominantly on intensity of feeling
of a religious nature, the worship of an absolute and the
giving of oneself to this absolute. In the case of the League
this was strict Roman Catholicism, for the Nazis race, for
the Bolsheviks marxism-leninism. The second phase is when
the society is rigidly structured into orders, when the new
social classification has become institutionalised and the
social hierarchy is arranged not according to purely emotional fervour or faith, but according to an adherence on
principle to the very substance of the faith, to the basic
principle of that society. We might look at the French
League as an illustration of these two phases. Of all the
numerous works on the subject of the second League the
one that throws most light on its nature is without a doubt
the *Dialogue d'entre le maheustre et le manant* printed in 1594,
attributed either to a M. Roland, aid to the Court of Moneys[2]
or to a M. L. Morin called Cromé judge at the Great
Council[3], both of whom were members of the famous Council
of Sixteen in Paris[4]. The *manant* (yokel) represents the Leaguer
while the *maheustre* (swaggerer) represents the royalist
supporter of Henry IV.

The League is a party of God's chosen ones who, guided by
the Holy Spirit, recruit by co-opting more members in order
to ensure that pure and ardent Roman Catholicism triumphs
in France over any heresy or lack of zeal.

'The Leaguer: God was helped in founding and starting
off the League of Catholics in Paris by the late Monsieur de
la Rocheblond, a citizen[5] of that town . . . inspired by God's
spirit he approached several Doctors, Priests and Preachers
to find out the way to govern there with an easy conscience
and for the public weal'. The people consulted were Prévôt,
priest of the parish of Saint-Séverin, Boucher, vicar of
Saint-Benoît, and Mathieu de Launay, canon of Soissons.
'These four men, having invoked the Holy Spirit, nominated
a few special Citizens': the advocate of Orléans, Messrs. de

Caumont (advocate), de Compans (merchant), Mignager (advocate), Crueé (procurator or attorney), de Manoeuvre ('of the house of Hennequin') and Deffiat ('a gentleman from the Auvergne country'). Then some time afterwards they chose other men among whom was 'the representative Roland', that is, a financial official in the Paris election, a tribunal concerned with assessing taxes throughout the countryside, the town being exempt from these, and with judging disputes. In all there were about twenty men.

However, they lost no time in laying the foundations of their organisation. The brain of the party was a secret council of nine or ten people who consulted and made all decisions together. The others were intelligence, recruitment and executive officers. Spread over the different districts of Paris and mingling with its citizens, they reported back to the council what they had heard 'and having heard events related, the council deliberated on the steps to take according to the circumstances'. They cultivated 'upright men' 'and according to the way their inclinations seemed to lie, they disclosed themselves to them without, however, saying anything about their assembly and if they elicited from them a measure of resoluteness and got to know their strength of purpose they reported this back to the small council." The secret council examined 'the life, habits and reputation of the people about whom they had heard'. If the examination was favourable then the council's agents 'issued their instructions to those with whom they had spoken, according to their station and informed them of what they had to do'. The secret council was therefore like the leaven in the lump, and this was the role of the party.

The leading council agents, five of them, later six, were joined by aides to form the famous Paris Council of Sixteen which alone was known publicly but which acted 'under the instructions of their (secret) council whom they (the sixteen) obeyed'.[6] The party covered France with a centralised network. 'Thereupon some upright citizens of Paris, all men of intelligence, were deputed to go, fully instructed, into various Provinces and Towns of the Kingdom and make some of the most ardent Catholics living in these towns themselves able to create and organise the League and develop it . . . so that there was only one body governed by a common intelligence throughout the whole of France.'[7] The provinces and towns sent agents to Paris who reported to the secret council and took orders from it. 'The Delegates from other towns were governed by this same council and received their instructions from it.'[8]

Under the direction of the secret council, the Sixteen in Paris and the comparable councils in other towns carried out the function of a kind of collective attorney-general requiring from all traditional institutions and every person serving them, whatever seemed to them in the public interest. First of all, from March 1587 onwards, they gave notice of what they were doing to the Catholic princes, Henri de Guise, his brother the Cardinal of Bourbon and the Duke of Mayenne, because only princes of royal blood could, in this society, give them legitimacy and provide the might of their dependant noblemen at arms. The Catholic princes and the League both swore to live and die together. More than one year in advance they prepared for the day of the Barricades which in 1588 forced Henry III to flee from his capital.

After the Barricades on 12 May 1588, there was no longer a king nor any magistrates. Two days afterwards, the Sixteen with the consent of Henri de Guise called a general assembly at the Hôtel de Ville and had elected 'according to the ancient Freedom'[9] provosts of Merchants and municipal Magistrates. Through these magistrates the Sixteen removed from office the colonels and captains of the militia and the quartermasters 'favouring the party of heresy and tyranny', and had others put in their place. 'Every day, they (the Sixteen) held council with the Prince and the Magistrates on what was to be done . . . and governed all the people through the will of God.' 'Through their Council', the prince sent dispatches in his name and in the name of the town of Paris, to all the provinces and towns and to His Holiness the Pope. Thus the Sixteen functioned as a medium for initiating, stimulating and controlling affairs.

After the assassination of the Catholic princes, Henri de Guise and the Cardinal de Guise, on the 23 and 24 December 1588, because the provosts of Merchants and Magistrates were detained at the States-General in Blois, there were no longer any magistrates in Paris. Thereupon the Sixteen got the people to take up arms, called a general assembly at the Hôtel de Ville, and had elected governor the Duke of Aumale the only Catholic prince present in Paris. On 16 January 1589 they had the most suspect magistrates in the Paris Parlement imprisoned and at the Hôtel de Ville had elected a coadjutor and two replacements for the provost of Merchants and municipal Magistrates, an advocate, a procurator and a merchant. Up to then they had, come what may, stayed within the framework of traditional institutions and simply filled them with their own men. But they felt the need to create their own public institutions, geared to their own objectives. 'Having done this they had the people elect a general Council of the Catholics' Union made up of three estates', the nobility, the clergy and the common folk. The delegates from the provinces and towns were entitled to speak and vote at the council when they came to Paris.[10] On this Council, which decided on matters for the whole of France, the Sixteen carried out the orders of the League's secret council. The Sixteen reported to the General Council of the Union on the state of the towns and provinces, made representations to prevent the liberation of prisoners, to disarm and put in prison 'political heretics and atheists', to prosecute certain traitors, to refuse small arms to heretics, to decline any attempts at negotiation or compromise and to have recourse to the King of Spain who provided them with generous help by way of men and money.

'At the same time special councils were established in each of the sixteen districts each one composed of nine distinguished persons elected by the ward.'[11]

Thus, a secret council, the brain and driving force being the League, public councils, the Paris Sixteen and other similar bodies elsewhere, made up of militants chosen by the secret council, and carrying out its orders, used their influence on their armed sympathisers in order to fill the traditional institutions either with their own men or with men of similar leanings, to whom orders were transmitted and courses of action suggested. They also put about the vague suggestion of a hierarchy of councils elected by the 'people', district councils, the General Council of the Catholics' Union, who likewise acted at the request and under the influence of the Sixteen and other public councils of the party. Therefore in fact, there was a dictatorship of the party, the League and its secret council but with some increasingly 'democratic' institutions, although the members of the district councils were 'distinguished men' and the general council consisted of three bishops, five priests, a canon, seven noblemen, but twenty-two commoners. There was a 'democracy' in the sense that these were bodies whose members were elected to power and did not acquire it by inheritance, by virtue of their function or by nomination from on high. Moreover this democracy was authoritarian, as all power was contained within these various bodies. However, it was a dictatorial democracy governed by an elite drawn from the party; 'The Catholics having no King, it was necessary to use an Aristocracy to govern and uphold the affairs of the Catholics' Union'.[12]

By what criterion did an individual become part of the League's secret council, the Council of Sixteen, the district councils, the General Council of the Union of Catholics or of

the traditional institutions 'according to the ancient freedom'? By dint of the strength of religious feeling, of faith in
Roman Catholicism and giving himself totally to the task of
ensuring its victory over 'heresy'. The fervour of feeling is one
of God's blessings so God can therefore bestow this freely,
according to His will, without the chosen one having any
particular merit whatever the origins or rank of the individual, for God takes shepherds in the field from their flocks
and makes them judges and kings. 'The Leaguer: Have you
noticed that the League gets its origins and its behaviour by
extraordinary means, both by God's own hand and because
He leads those who serve Him by the hand, as He led the
people of Israel in the Middle of Egypt and its deserts . . .?'
The supporters of the League were 'moved by God's spirit'.
They march under the guidance of the Holy Spirit, God
sustains them and protects them against the king, leads them
by the hand and, by a string of miracles enables them to
resist 'a tyrant King', 'a heretic King'. 'Against all mortal
hope they resisted both one and the other, O God, sole
creator of such ventures.' Intensity of faith extends even to
the final sacrifice of lives and possessions. 'It was the first
resolution at the beginning of the League that one should
reconcile oneself to death and embark upon it resolutely.'
'All those entering the League used their possessions and
wealth for it and renounced their lives.'[13]

The programme embarked upon was the triumph of pure
Roman Catholicism throughout the whole of France, the
state, orders, corporate bodies, provinces and towns:

'The preservation of the Apostolic, Roman Catholic
Religion; . . . fighting and driving out heresy and sects
opposed to the Catholic Religion . . . the reform of vice,
impiousness, injustice and other ills in all the Estates of
France: and bringing piety and justice to bear where
impiousness and tyranny prevail.'

The criterion of strength of faith led to institutions being transformed first of all by encumbering the existing political and administrative institutions with bodies like the council of Sixteen, the district councils, or with special agents responsible for influencing their operation, then by filling these institutions with men of proven sentiments through establishing or re-establishing elections conducted according to 'democratic' principles, and finally by creating new 'democratic' public institutions based on the principle of controlled elections. Power was taken away from everyone who did not show evidence of sufficient intensity of faith. 'The Leaguer: The obedience I have sworn to Princes and Magistrates goes as far as the altar and no further. For if they do things contrary to my religion, I will neither obey nor serve them.'[14]

'The true inheritors of the Crown are those who are worthy of bearing God's nature. If it pleases God to give us a king of French nationality, blessed be his name; if a king from Lorraine, blessed be his name; if a Spaniard or a German, blessed be his name. We care nothing of his nationality, *provided he is a Catholic full of piety and justice*, because we have no preference for the nation but for the religion . . . I would prefer to be a Spanish Catholic and practise my religion and find salvation than a French heretic losing my immortal soul; and I tell you that I love my native France and love to practise my religion there, but without my religion, I no longer would wish to live there.'[15]

Thus the source of legitimate, legal power is purity and strength of faith: 'being Catholic and full of piety and justice'. Likewise this is the source of the nation and the source of an international party whose frontiers transcend nations and which rejects any materialist society: 'The Spaniards and Italians', France's enemies in so many wars

since Charles VIII went down into Italy in 1494, 'now are
our brothers and friends in religion. Just as they are my
enemy *over goods and possessions* so they are my close and
favoured friend in the matter of Religion. For the well-born
person prefers his religion *to any other possession* whatever it
may be.'[16]

However if the criterion of strength of faith was destined
to upset the whole political organisation, it also was to lead
to a revolution in society. The Leaguers did not suspect that
there would be a move away from an order-based society
towards another type of society. They could not conceive of
another type of society. They wanted to retain the structure of
clergy, nobility and commoners. But for them the nobleman
was to be a man to whom God had given great strength of
faith. Leaguers distinguished between the 'bad nobility
following the path of heresy' (a 'mad nobility') and the 'good
nobility' practising the pure Catholic faith. The bad nobility
was refused by the Catholic population, all rank, honour and
allegiance: 'So long as the Nobility follows the party of
heresy or wants to tyrannise the people, the people will show
them neither favour nor allegiance: but if, on the other
hand, it is willing to unite against heresy . . . then you will
see all the people honour them, and dutifully grant them
their devotion . . .' But it was necessary to go further than
this. In actual fact, what made a nobleman was strength of
faith and one could easily conclude from this that the
hierarchy within the ranks of the nobility depended on the
degree of strength of faith.

'The Leaguer: The general species of Nobility *is based
solely on the qualities one acquires not on those inherited* from
someone else; and the title of Nobility *should be a
personal one and not a hereditary* matter, so that a person of
no quality cannot be Noble; and I ask you to believe
that in our experience over thirty or forty years, the

Nobility is at present only an imaginary species, and quite ineffectual, the fault proceeding simply from this fact : that *your children are satisfied with their race and do not seek the path of virtue*, and there have been, as there still are, more tyrannical monsters than virtuous and valiant nobility.'

The Leaguer was joining here a theoretician Jehan de Caumont whose book had been published in 1585 and by which he perhaps was inspired.[17] Caumont wrote:

'The man who displays the most excellent behaviour among his kind should be ranked as the most noble . . . Behaviour which is proper, essential and natural to man and in accordance with the purpose of his creation . . . is to glorify God, behave in accordance with God, show his image in the Majesty of a second God . . . *Thus those who honour God the most and who take the greatest pains to see that he is honoured are the true noblemen and gentry* . . . Take away from the nobility the honouring of God and you take away from it its very being : take away virtue and you take away life, it dies straightaway . . . A heretic was never noble, they are all liars, villains, cowards and faint-hearted. The Catholic is truly Noble . . .'

Thus those and only those who have proved the strength of their Catholic faith could be gentlemen and noblemen, and the stronger their faith the more noble could they be. The majority of French nobility would be replaced by another one, springing from the ranks of the League, and graded according to the importance of their role in the League, since this role was directly related to strength of faith. Those with the most important roles because their faith was the most powerful and vigorous, were the members of the secret Council who would be put at the top of the new hierarchy of noblemen. There was still a nobility but the guiding principle behind it and the basic organisational principle of society were completely changed. Other consequences which the Leaguers had not perhaps thought of resulted from this. As nobility and degree of nobility depended on strength of faith, the nobility not only became personal, non-hereditary, open to everyone at all times and therefore eminently 'democratic', in a certain sense, but in addition it and its rank became temporary. In fact an individual, depending on how his own faith varied in intensity, since this intensity could not remain constant over a whole lifetime, or according to how the faith of others varied in intensity, outstripping or being outstripped by him, this same individual could acquire or lose nobility, change rank within the nobility several times during his life. Social mobility therefore became very common within a totally fluid society, and, practically speaking within this order-based society with a very hierarchic structure, there was a high degree of social equality.

However, although the League lasted only a very short time, one can see already the outlines of the second phase in which the social hierarchy is no longer organised according to strength of feeling for a religious faith but rather according to one's adherence on principle to the very substance of faith, and this adherence can be of an intellectual, rational and non-zealous kind. People with fervour are always a minority and never numerous enough to embrace the whole of society. They have to use less ardent people who are far more numerous and who previously had power and influence within society, and come to terms with them. This is what happened to the Leaguers. They had to come to an understanding with the Catholic princes. When the Leaguers formed the General Council of the Union, the princes forced them to add to the forty members they had had elected, fourteen other members among whom were the presidents of the Royal Courts, Janin, Le Maistre, d'Ormesson and

Videville, as well as the two Villeroys, both Secretaries of State. These magistrates and state councillors were inclined to be moderate. They had a number of imprisoned heretics freed and gave heart to the moderates.

The 'Catholic' princes and eminent men had fully appreciated the political and social revolution embodied in the League's activities and ideas, and though they wanted Catholicism to triumph, they did not want this revolution to come about. They 'spread the rumour that the Sixteen wanted to bring down the French Monarchy to a popular Estate'[18] and they alienated from the purist Leaguers a good number of people of all 'estates'. The 'Catholic' princes had force of arms at their disposal. The Duke of Mayenne, the chief official of the League, took all knowledge of its affairs out of the hands of the General Council of the Union and gave it to a special council made up of his own followers who disregarded all the Sixteen's requests. The 'Catholic' provinces and towns ceased to send their representatives to the General Council. The Union crumbled. Paris again came under the sway of the Parlement. The 'Catholics' returned to the traditional rigid order-based society, even before the victory of Henry IV re-established social and political order in the kingdom.

3. *General theory of development of societies of orders*

If we compare the League to the French Republic of 1793, Italian Fascism, German Nazism, or Russian Bolshevism we can outline a general theory on the two phases of all order-based societies. The first period is when the society is being established, its very beginnings, when the new social stratification that is being sketched out under the influence of an organised and hierarchically structured party, is being established chiefly on the strength of feelings of a religious nature, on the worship of an absolute and the sacrifice of the individual to this absolute. For the League this was strict Roman Catholicism, for the Nazis it was race, for the Bolsheviks marxism-leninism. The people in the highest social positions are henceforth those with the most fervent, ardent and unalloyed faith in the party's doctrine. In each case the result is a society composed of orders because social classification derives from the honour, dignity and rank attached to strength of feelings not from hereditary religious purity (castes) or from the part played in the production of material goods (classes). This kind of society of orders is moreover decidedly democratic, mobile and fluid. It is democratic because anyone, whatever his birth and origins, can reach a level of intense feelings, borne out by his actions, and thereby be classified among the highest ranks of the social hierarchy. Social mobility both upwards and downwards is very pronounced because the individual can, in a short space of time, climb, up or down the social ladder. Society is also extremely fluid as it is perpetually changing. In fact, an individual might go up or down the social hierarchy several times either because his own strength of feeling varies or because that of his fellow men and comrades in arms varies. When their strength of feeling grows and is socially acknowledged, they rise higher in the hierarchy in relation to the individual in question, and conversely, when their strength of feeling declines and this is socially recognised, they drop down the hierarchy in relation to it. This kind of society corresponds to an authoritarian and dictatorial democratic state, or at least to an authoritarian and dictatorial government of a state which could have been of a different sort.

No society of orders based on strength of feeling of a religious character, or strength of faith in a vision of the world and society has lasted. Among the least ephemeral of them, the outlines of a rigid kind of order-based society just began to take shape. The longest lasting, in Soviet Russia, is gradually being changed into a rigid type of order structure despite periodic fluctuations. The society of orders based on strength of feeling is therefore not a special type of society of orders but a stage in the movement from one society to another. The first phase serves to break up the previous society be it a society of orders based on another principle or a class-based society, in order to allow movement towards either a society of orders based on a new principle of classification following on a change in the scale of moral and social values, or towards a class-based society.

In each case, the party may envisage a complete transformation of society according to the logic of its principle: that of intense feelings attached to matter of faith. But it may also seek to secure the predominance of its principle while at the same time preserving the society in which it lives, by encumbering every 'estate', every body, every institution with a watchdog group recruited according to the principle of intensity of faith and which imposes the party's decision and control on each 'estate' and on the operation of all the institutions. In the long run, when a party has control in this way it ought to lead to a transformation of society.

The principle of social classification according to strength of feelings cannot therefore bring about an instantaneous or rapid transformation of the structure of society. It can leave behind traces of the old order for some time, while radically changing the way it operates, if it infiltrates every social stratum and every institution with a control-group sprung from a party that is recruited and graded according to the principle of strength of feelings.

However, this first phase, this period of fluidity where everything is based on strength of feeling, cannot last. It gives way, within a few years, twenty or thirty at most, to the second phase, the period of social rigidity in which orders and 'estates' are organised into the classic and inflexible form of order-based society where the social hierarchy is no longer structured according to strength of feelings or degree of faith but according to the degree of adherence to the substance of faith, to the basic principle of society. The transition from one phase to the next is brought about initially as a result of the need to have within every institution competent men well versed in administrative and political matters and procedures, even if the strength of their faith has fallen off. This phenomenon is a process of bureaucratisation or something analogous to it. Concurrently there is a tendency within each and every man to ensure his own security during this lifetime, hence the stability of his social status as well as his social rank, and the immutable nature of his function. Lastly every family man tends to want to guarantee his children a status and rank in society at least equal to his own if needs be through a different social function that is equal or superior to his own, if not through the same social function as his own, through the same profession with the same grade. With these three factors operating, the fluid society becomes a classic, rigidly-structured society of orders with its particular characteristics, its fixed ranks, and firm hierarchies and their marks of honour, their privileges, their freedoms and all their distinctive characteristics.

Notes to Chapter Five

1. Liturgical in the original Greek sense: "work for the people".
2. A sovereign court for the preservation of currency standards and the supervision of the Mint. Half of these aides toured the country as inspectors, half sat in Paris assisting Judges of the Court.
3. The supreme Court of Appeal on benefices, judgements of the municipal council and certain other courts.
4. *Dialogue d'entre le maheustre et le manant* as an appendix to the Satyre Ménipée, Editions de Ratisbonne, for the estate of Mathias Kerner, 1726, Vol. 3: *Preuves de la Satyre Ménipée*, pp. 367–585, in Bibliothèque Nationale in Paris, LB 36–456H.
5. Legally speaking, a 'citizen of Paris' (a '*bourgeois de Paris*') was someone living in Paris, paying municipal taxes, participating in the militia; he was awarded this title by the municipal magistrates. But socially a *bourgeois de*

Paris was a rentier or a 'financier', that is someone involved in farming of royal taxes and public credit operations.

6. Op. cit, p. 448.
7. *Ibid.*, p. 419.
8. *Ibid.*, p. 448.
9. *Ibid.*, p. 446.
10. *Ibid.*, p. 453, p. 472.
11. *Ibid.*, p. 454
12. *Ibid.*, p. 481.
13. *Ibid.*, pp. 433, 434, 438, 443, 445, 446.
14. *Ibid.*, p. 539.
15. *Ibid.*, p. 561, 564.
16. *Ibid.*, p. 560.
17. *De la vertu de noblesse, aux roys et princes très chrestiens*, Paris, by Frédéric Morel, Ordinary Printer to the King 1585, with the permission of the said Lord, Bib. Nat. D29406 pp. 2–5.
18. *Ibid.*, p. 483.

Chapter Six

The Military Order: France in the sixteenth and seventeenth centuries

One constantly comes back to Charles Loyseau, the magistrate who in 1610 published a kind of anatomy of French society in the sixteenth and seventeenth centuries. This was reprinted many times, until, in the eighteenth century, attention was focussed on the society of classes during its formation.[1] In the *Traité des Ordres et simples dignitez* (Treatise on Orders and Common Ranks) we see that Loyseau believes the whole of French society to be split into hierarchically graded orders. Order is 'rank with natural ability in public office', 'and in French it is called especially "estate" as it is the most durable rank and quality inseparable from a man'. This rank 'of the same kind and with the same title, belongs to several persons',[2] 'several' at that time meaning in French not 'a few' but indeed 'a great many'. With the order then we are dealing with a social group.

French society was officially divided into three principal orders. At the top was the ecclesiastical order, the clergy, for by rights the 'ministers of God' should retain 'the first rank of honour'.[3] Then comes the nobility, either 'aristocracy' 'ancient and immemorial' sprung from 'an ancient line' or nobility of rank deriving from high office or seigniories which conferred the same privileges.[4] Lastly the third estate which encompassed the rest of the people.[5]

However, each of these principal orders sub-divides into 'special orders' structured into 'ranks', 'degrees' or 'minor orders'.[6] The ecclesiastical order includes the following hierarchy, listed in descending order of importance: cardinals; primates or patriarchs; archbishops; the three sacred orders of priests; deacons; subdeacons; the four minor

67

orders of acolytes; exorcists; lectors; gate-keepers; and finally clerics or 'tonsured ones', for 'the tonsure . . . is the way of entry into all the ecclesiastical orders and it is this which makes a cleric distinct from the rest of the populace'.[7] The order of nobility sub-divides into, from highest to lowest: princes of the blood; princes; more distant family of the sovereign;[8] the high nobility of knights[9] distinguishable one from another by their fiefs of rank; in descending order, duke, marquis, count, baron, castellans,[10] lastly the ordinary strain of aristocrats, all bearing arms.[11] The third estate includes in fact legal and financial officials, although some of these might be noblemen of high office or rank.[12] As a general rule, at the head of this order came 'men of learning', doctors, masters and bachelors of the Faculties of Theology, Jurisprudence, Medicine and Arts (grammar, rhetoric and philosophy). Then came the lawyers followed by the financiers 'all those concerned with handling finance, that is the king's funds'. Next were the 'practitioners or executive officers', wearers of the long robe, clerks, notaries, procurators, then wearers of the short robe, sergeants, trumpeters, official valuers, vendors. After them came the merchants 'as much for the public usefulness even necessity of trade . . . as for the usual wealth of merchants, which wins them great credit and respect, added to which the means they have of employing artisans and manual workers secures for them much power in the towns: so the merchants are last among the people bearing a title of honour, being called "honourable men" or "worthy people" and "bourgeois of the towns" '. Together with them are ranked the trades of apothecary, goldsmith, jeweller, haberdasher, 'wholesaler', draper, hosier, furrier as belonging more to trade than manual labour. All the foregoing can bear the title of *'bourgeois'* if they live in the privileged towns having corporate and community rights, if they share in the honours of the city; its rights and privileges, and if they have a voice in its assemblies. Then, below the merchants, come all those employed in trades 'which depend more on bodily labour than on the trade of goods or cleverness of mind and these are the lowliest'. They are, firstly, the farm workers 'those whose normal occupation is working the land for others such as tenant farmers'. The latter, like all village people or 'peasants' are 'lowly people'. Below them, however, are ranked artisans or craftsmen '. . . who practise the mechanical arts as they are called as distinct from the liberal arts . . . We commonly call mechanical what is lowly and abject . . .' with their qualifications of master, guild member and apprentice. Still lower down the scale come 'those who have neither craft nor trade and who earn their livelihood through the strength of their arm. These we call therefore hands or hirelings such as the carriers who help masons, carters and other casual workers are the lowliest of common folk', of the towns and countryside. Lastly, at the foot of the social ladder is the order of 'able-bodied beggars', 'vagabonds and tramps' who live 'in idle and carefree fashion, at the expense of others'.[3]

Every order has 'its distinctive mark, badge or visible ornament', in other words its social symbols. Members of the ecclesiastical order wear the long robe and have their hair tonsured. Furthermore members of the four minor orders wear the surplice or the alb; sub-deacons have the fanon or maniple on the left arm; deacons the stole; priests the chasuble; bishops the mitre, crozier, gloves and ring; cardinals have their hat and scarlet robe. 'Among the nobles, the ordinary gentlefolk have their coats of arms; knights have gilded spurs and harness . . . princes wear a prince's cloak . . . Among the commoners, doctors, masters and bachelors have their hoods of various kinds, according to their different faculties, as well as the long robe which they have in common with the ecclesiastics; advocates their cornet-shaped hats; procurators have just the long robe which distinguishes them from the ordinary legal practitioners who have no power to administer justice . . .'

Orders hold 'two other prerogatives of honour, namely title and rank'. Titles are those of *chevalier* for great noblemen, important crown officials, members of the Council of State, presidents and king's men at the Parlement in Paris, the leading presidents at other sovereign courts. Then there is *noble homme* for officers of the law and advocates who are not of the nobility and *damoiselle* for their wives. 'Councillor of the King' is used for numerous officials, members of the Parlements, magistrates, seneschals, their lieutenants, and chief treasurers of France. There are the 'epithets of honour', 'illustrious and most excellent' for princes, 'mighty and powerful lord' for chevaliers and great noblemen, 'most illustrious' for cardinals, 'most reverend' for bishops, 'Reverend Father in God' for abbots, 'venerable and discreet person' for other lesser ecclesiastics, 'honoured sir' for officers, 'honourable man' or 'worthy person' for the bourgeois.

There were particular styles : '*sire*' for the King, '*monseigneur*' for the prince, '*messire*' for the knight, '*monsieur*' for the ordinary nobleman, '*maistre*' for the man of letters, '*sire* so-and-so' for the merchant or craftsman, '*madame*' for the wife of a knight, '*mademoiselle*' for a nobleman's wife, '*dame* so-and-so' or by licence '*madame* 'for the wife of a bourgeois.[14]

Every order has its 'rank, which is the precedence in sitting and walking', 'namely the ecclesiastical order first, then the nobility, then the third estate : although there is no statutory order', only 'voluntary respect'. The humblest priest therefore should precede the most elevated of the ordinary nobility.

'But because the ecclesiastical order is considered an extraordinary order that is outside the realm of temporal affairs, our Redeemer having Himself said that his Kingdom was not of this world . . . it can nowadays frequently be observed that those men possessing a degree of secular rank are unwilling to give way to priests if these do not have some degree of ecclesiastical rank'.

'The humblest gentleman should precede the wealthiest and most honourable member of the third estate.'

But a difficulty arises if the member of the third estate is a king's officer. In this case, princes 'give way to no officers whoever they may be'; knights and other members of the high nobility only give way to officers who are also knights because of their offices 'as these have the same order as themselves and their office in addition', such as the Chancellor of France, councillors of the Council of State, heads of the sovereign courts; ordinary noblemen, gentlemen, and squires give way to the king's officers who are magistrates, that is the chief government and legal officials, 'in their depth and extent of their power', even if they are commoners.

The orders have no power, no public administrative organisation. But some of them 'have corporate entity and colleges which sometimes have the privilege of being able to make statutes and elect senior officials who have jurisdiction over the whole body', or include organised bodies and colleges such as the guilds.[15]

Orders have certain privileges. Only gentlemen have the right to wear a coat of arms surmounted with a helmet or 'head armour'. A certain number of offices are reserved on principle for gentlemen: senior officers of the King's Household, many military offices, gentlemen of the Privy Chamber, gentlemen and servants of the Royal Household, equerries of the stable, gentlemen of the hunt and falconry. 'All the principal military appointments either in command of fortresses or of companies, in particular all cavalry commands and even the lowest places in the king's regiments,[16] as also captaincies of infantry, gentlemen are given preference.'

For ecclesiastical appointments 'several' (that is 'many') churches, cathedrals, 'several' abbeys have their positions of rank, canonries and religious places reserved for gentlemen. In general, gentlemen are favoured in the church by dispensations as regards plurality of benefices or time devoted to study. As regards manorial domains, the fiefs are reserved for gentlemen. Commoners can only acquire them by dispensation and by paying the king a free-fief charge. But only gentlemen can hold large and medium-sized domains—dukedoms, marquisates, and shires on the one hand and baronies, viscountcies, vidameships, and castellaries, on the other. Commoners can only acquire small domains and high, middle or low judgeships.

Gentlemen, to the exclusion of nobles of the long robe, alone have the right to carry the sword 'as the mark and emblem of the nobility, and in France it is worn even in the King's Chamber'. All members of the high nobility have the right to be saluted by commoners. Offering their lives in the defence of the State, the gentlemen are 'exempt from taxes and all other personal contributions levied in war time . . . and from billeting soldiers'. 'Gentlemen have besides the privilege of hunting . . . so that in peacetime they keep to a form of exercise resembling war'.

For an ordinary crime, gentlemen are not punished as severely as commoners and are never condemned to degrading punishment such as the whip or the noose. However, while the nobility receive relatively light corporal punishment, they are more fiercely treated in monetary terms. And for crimes repugnant to the nobility such as treason, larceny, perjury and fraudulent behaviour, which are aggravated by the rank of the person, they are more severely punished.

Gentlemen enjoy the privilege of obtaining satisfaction for an insult by duel. But duelling is exclusively for them. They are not bound to fight duels with commoners.[17]

The third estate benefits from a great general privilege,

namely that gentlemen, with the exception of glassmakers and a few others, cannot take part in trades or crafts for the purposes of gain, cannot in fact compete with the third estate.[18]

An order is something acquired. The ecclesiastical order is entered by way of the tonsure which bears public witness to the fact that a man is dedicating himself to God. The order of nobility is entered by birth or by letters patent from the King, 'God's appointed dispenser of the substantial honours of this world',[19] or by appointment to, acceptance of and installation in those ennobling offices, be they royal or municipal. In this way senior officers of the Crown, head officials in the King's Household, heads of sovereign courts, the King's governors and lieutenants in the provinces become knights and therefore members of the high nobility. Since they belong to the high nobility, their children acquire nobility. The secretaries to the King, Household and Crown of France have the nobility of four generations and their nobility passes to their children provided they resign in favour of a son or son-in-law. Councillors of the sovereign courts have a personal title of nobility but if a grandfather, son and grandson have held office uninterruptedly nobility passes to their descendants. By royal privilege, the municipal offices of certain towns confer nobility on their holders. Lastly, any person can be recognised as a nobleman through the pronouncement of the Board of Excise if he can prove that he, his father and his grandfather have lived as noblemen, preferably with a manor or fief, exercising the profession of arms, and have never committed any action that was unworthy of their rank. Later on, these conditions had to be augmented by a royal declaration on 22 June 1664 which required authentic evidence of nobility dating to before 1560.[20]

Orders within the third estate are acquired by receiving university degrees, by appointment to, acceptance and installation in different offices, by enrolment as an advocate or attorney in the various courts of justice, by being accepted in a craft guild.[21]

Membership of an order can be lost too. The priest's order is taken away in the rare event of unfrocking for infamy.[22] Nobility of rank can be lost through infamy which entails being deprived of office. Nobility of blood is lost through *lèse-majesté* or treason, when the gentleman is declared infamous and dismissed from the nobility by being thus condemned. But other crimes and the exercise of base mechanical arts for gain, do not eradicate the nobility of gentlemen but simply suspend it, because nobility of blood is 'as it were, natural to a man'. If the lapsed nobleman recommences his noble way of life, it is enough for him to obtain from the king letters of rehabilitation which the king never refuses. The gentleman could even do without this, as 'it is a common rule that rights of blood and nature cannot be lost by civil means'.

'The functions not compatible with the nobility are those of procurator acting for another, registrar, notary, sergeant, clerk, merchant and craftsmen of every trade . . . . This is understandable when these functions are carried out for gain, because it is base, sordid gain which derogates from nobility, the proper way of life of which is living on one's rents and not selling one's effort and labour. However, judges, advocates, doctors and professors of liberal sciences do not derogate from the nobility they otherwise possess although they earn their living by means of their position, because (apart from the fact that it derives from intellectual and not manual work) it is honourable rather than mercenary . . . Farming does not detract from nobility . . . in as much as no occupation pursued by a gentleman for himself and not involving taking money from others detracts from nobility . . . it is not forbidden for nobles to hold share-cropping leases (métaires) in perpetuity, over a long period of years or for life; because in these leases the useful title seigniory of the land is transferred to the tenant . . . with the result that henceforth the gentleman is said to be cultivating his own land and not that of another man . . .'[23]

This is the picture that Loyseau paints of the stratification into orders of French society. This lawyer describes for us particularly what had gained legal value from custom, edicts, ordinances, and decrees of the Council and the Courts of Parlement. Although his book is strewn with penetrating observations taken from everyday life, this writer does not give us a complete sociological description. (And we do not reproach him for this.) He does not stress the tendency towards endogamy at all levels of the two lay orders, which is compensated for by cases of exogamy; the general tendency towards heredity within the order or estate and the caste tendencies that take shape among the gentility; the restrictions on social mobility that derive from customs and manners, for often several generations of living as a gentleman were needed for the ennobled to be considered by the gentry as part of their social group. It is not surprising that Loyseau does not stress one essential principle because to him it was obvious, that a family is not ranked among the higher levels of this hierarchy through money acquired in activities involving the production of material goods, industry, commerce, and agriculture, if carried on in order to sell the produce. It is the order to which one belongs which determines the amount of worldly wealth one receives; for the clergy, the nobility and the higher levels of the third estate this will be in the form of rents, seigniorial income, ground rents, government annuities by way of pensions, allowances, bonds, fees, including *douceurs*, proportional grants or 'taxations'. Even remuneration for production-oriented activities is sometimes regulated by customs and habits rather than the state of the market. In fact, there were poor gentlemen, poor graduates and poor magistrates but they were, generally speaking, held in higher esteem than the richest of merchants.

Many other works throw more light on what Loyseau has already shown. Legally speaking, the order of nobility was second in importance, though socially speaking it came first and was the order to which everyone aspired. Officials, bourgeois, and merchants were called *sieur*, adopted the title of 'esquire' the first one that a gentleman could bear. Their wives assumed the name '*demoiselle*'. The husbands also put a helmet on their coats of arms despite the fact that the ordinances of Orléans and Blois forbade this, they bore a sword and dressed in the style of gentlemen. A contemporary of Loyseau, Montchrestien, in his *Traité de l'économie politique* of 1615 bewailed the fact that 'It is currently quite impossible to tell the difference from appearances. The shop-keeper is dressed like the gentleman . . . Moreover, who can be unaware that this conformity in self-adornment heralds the corruption of our age-old discipline?' By exercising the profession of arms, by living a noble life on manors and fiefs, and especially by holding ennobling offices, members of the higher levels of the third estate succeeded in being legally recognised as noble, with all the privileges of gentlemen. However, socially these nobles were not gentlemen. Men of the sword refused to recognise them as such. They even refused them the title of nobles of rank, function or robe. For noblemen of the sword, gentlemen of the robe were nothing but 'burgesses' (bourgeois).[24] Their feelings are very well expressed by a character in a novel:

'I do not know by what mischance most of those people (i.e. Councillors of Parlement) go half mad in their old age . . . the most likely reasons are, firstly, that they are persons of a base nature, being born as they are of the most humble parents, and that in order to keep their absurd dignity they shut themselves off from good company and only spend their time on things that make them all the more stupid as they are the most despicable people in the world.'[25]

The son of an ennobled person whom the gentlemen of Angoumois must have recognised however, in 1649, as having the 'quality' of a gentleman, Jean-Louis Guez de Balzac, wrote to Chapelain on 20 December 1636:

'I have the utmost regard for the person of our friend and would fervently wish to bring about the union of our two houses. But . . . the young lady's head is full of her nobility, hence her scorn of any kind of bourgeois were he robed in purple and seated on a cloth of fleurs de lys. Her mother would have less elevated thoughts, and be more favourably disposed towards the long robe . . . (but) . . . she is daily solicited by numerous people of high standing; and, according to the feelings she expressed yesterday when I saw her, a Councillor of the Great Council would not be enough for her daughter.'[26]

Bourgeois! That was all this nobility of the robe represented for the gentry. The abbé Francois-Timoléon de Choisy, a member of the French Academy, went further still: 'My mother, who was of the house of Hurault de l'Hospital often said to me:

'Listen, my son. Don't be at all vainglorious and think of yourself *only as a bourgeois*. I am very well aware of the fact that your fathers and grandfathers were Masters of Requests, Councillors of State; but take it from me that in France, the only nobility that is recognised is nobility of the sword. It is a warlike nation and one that glorifies the profession of the arms.'[27]

The military character of the French society is emphasized

by the Archbishop of Embrun, messire Georges d'Aubusson
de la Feuillade, president of the Assembly of the Clergy, at
exactly the same time as the two *Cahiers de la noblesse* which
are quoted below, in the very middle of the Fronde, and in
the very year of the second of our texts, when he replied
thus on 15 March 1651 to the delegates at the assembly of
noblemen: 'Thus it is that nobility not of blood but of your
heroic spirits, not buried in the tombs of your ancestors but
living again through these your noble actions, that has
inspired you to assemble to preserve your privileges . . . It
is that ancient glory . . . which could no longer suffer all
the affairs of a State, *which is military in its very foundation* and
of which you form the most powerful and illustrious part,
to be decided without your assent.'[28]

The gentlemen pushed the noblemen of the robe outside
the nobility. It is noteworthy, too, that at the States-General
of 1614–15 the majority of noblemen of the robe sat among
the third estate. A struggle between orders thus dominated
French society. At the States-General of 1614–15, as a result
of a procedural stratagem by the government in the elections
of the third estate, the latter was in fact, 'the fourth estate',
i.e. that of men of the robe. It was the struggle of orders,
between the officials and the nobility that allowed the king to
remain the arbiter and brought about the failure of the
States-General.[29]

The order of the nobility blamed the higher levels of the
third estate for stepping outside their sphere of competence
and competing with them. They complained of the fact that,
by means of money earned in commerce or 'finance' members
of the third estate acquired fiefs and manors from noblemen
in debt and monopolised royal offices which from the time
of Francis I had been officially sold or given in return for
loans 'never to be repaid' and of which the reversions and,
especially since 1604, the annual due or *paulette*, an insurance
premium, were said to have been made hereditary. The

gentlemen called for the abolition of the annual due as well as the sale of offices. They asked for certain offices to be reserved exclusively for them and at least a third of all the others. Thus, they were asking, in short, for the maintenance of their social pre-eminence through their access to high ranking positions (office being 'rank together with a public function'), but also through their access to the emoluments, salaries, fees and taxations that went with offices. They even went further than this, and the members of the third estate were indignant because nobles were asking for authorisation to engage in big business in order to make money without detracting from their positions.

However, in such conditions, is it not money that classifies people in the social hierarchy, and are we not seeing a class-based society being formed? Is not the struggle between officials or men of the robe and the gentry a class struggle? I do not think so. There is evidence to suggest that at the level of merchants and farmers there is a class-structured society in the process of being formed and this does interfere with the statutory society through the development of commercial capitalism. But, when it comes to the level of men of the robe and the gentry, then it does still seem to be a matter of orders and conflicts between orders. Here are some of my reasons. Whatever the gentlemen claimed, money alone was not sufficient to enable a man to gain office in the judiciary. A grain merchant who had become rich would not have been able to buy an office as councillor in the Parlement either for himself, or, as often as not, for his son. Even if he had inveigled the Chancellor, he would not have been accepted by the sovereign Court. The humbleness of his origins would not have allowed this to happen. As a rule, it was necessary to rise up in the world little by little, moving from trading to finance, from finance to a junior office in the judiciary or as one of the king's secretaries. From there, one could aspire to the various offices of the magistracy, the seneschal's court or the sovereign courts, then those of the Master of Requests and the Council of State. As often as not, it took two, three, usually four generations to get this far. It was the quality accorded by a consensus of opinion to the way of life of each social station that allowed a man to rise higher and higher up the social scale, by means of the resources acquired from the level one had arrived at in the hierarchy of orders in the form of rents, salaries, and fees, not in the form of profits. The gentry were precluded from the judiciary less by lack of income than by the rash expenditure occasioned by their way of life as well as their contempt for education.

One might say the same of manors and fiefs. A grain merchant could well force a gentleman in his debt to sell him a fief in order to discharge his obligations (though more often gentlemen wanting to borrow money turned to officials who were higher-ranking in the social hierarchy). But the merchant was obliged to pay the free-fief, and possession of a fief was not enough to ennoble him. He was only tolerated, and was still liable to pay the *taille*. And only if he adopted the nobleman's way of life on his fief would he, or rather his son and more probably his grandson be able, after many years, to persuade the collectors to strike him off the list of those liable to pay the *taille* because for a long time he had lived nobly, his sword by his side, and without 'carrying on any trade'. Then it is worth noting that the noblemen of the robe did not particularly want to adopt the gentleman's way of life and assume the profession of arms and indulge in unbridled generosity. Some did do these things and it was then that they experienced the difficulties of the gentry and often brought about the downfall of their families. But, in general, it was rare, by a deliberate act of choice, to enter the nobility of the sword by the profession of arms and seek access to the higher ranks of the army and the governorship of fortified places or districts. It was more frequent for those

reaching the offices of Master of Requests or the commissions
of Councillor of State to establish their eldest sons in positions
in the Council of State with, for some families such as the
Phélypeaux, access to the highest positions of Secretary of
State, Comptroller, General of France, and Minister. However, the usual thing was to consolidate eldest sons in offices
in the Parlements which have 'something sacred and
venerable about them',[30] or in the offices of other sovereign
Courts such as the Nicolai family in the Chamber of Audit.
The sovereign courts, in addition to public esteem and the
peaceful existence of quiet, regular and routine functions,
offered possibilities for saving and increasing one's money,
business deals and commissions, loans, farming of taxes, land
deals, all of which were not offered by life in the royal army.
Consequently the majority of men of the robe preferred the
king's Council and the sovereign Courts, the high magistracy, with the members of all these bodies forming a single
social group, an order, with a nobility of function legally
similar to that of the gentry though socially distinct from it.
Between the gentry and the robe marriage ties were formed,
mostly due to exogamy on the part of the women. However, what mattered in this patrilineal society was the fate
of the men and particularly the eldest sons. One should not
be deceived by the younger sons of officials of the robe opting
for the profession of arms and by the junior branches of
official families of the robe carrying on this profession from
father to son. So long as a man did not succeed in rising
higher than the rank of colonel or gain important governorships, it was difficult to enter the gentry if one was not
born a gentleman. A family in which the eldest sons and the
senior branch remain men of the robe is a family of the robe.
As in all things, there can be exceptions.[31]

Generally speaking, men of the robe remained in their
order. Yet there is a constant, stubborn effort shown in the
attitudes and words of the third estate at the States-General

1614–15, by the policy of the Paris Parlement, by its role and the role of other parlements during the Fronde, not to change the society of orders into a class-based society but to change the hierarchy of orders so that the magistracy, 'the gentlemen of pen and ink', might be recognised as the highest order, to change the principle of society and get people to recognise as the most worthy occupation not the service of arms but the civil service of the state. The magistracy was to be recognised above all others, as the real and highest nobility. Loyseau expands on this tendency within French society very simply. He arranges everything in relation to fitness to exercise public power. So he divides society into two sectors, those who command and those who obey. Those who command are the king and the magistrates, his officials. Those who obey are the people, that is all the rest of the community, ecclesiastics, nobles and the third estate.

'The sovereign has his general officers close to him. They dispatch his orders to provincial magistrates who in turn convey them to town magistrates[32] and the latter have them carried out by the people. This is then, how we have those who command and the people who obey, because these are a body with several heads divided into orders, estates or particular occupations. Some are dedicated especially to the service of God, others to protecting the State by force of arms; others to providing its food and sustaining it by peaceful occupations. These are our three orders of States-General of France: clergy, nobility and the third estate.'[33]

So far as Loyseau was concerned, it was not merely a matter of magistrates simply having authority in the exercise of their functions by virtue of powers delegated by the king, but also of social pre-eminence. In fact, Loyseau stresses that princes being closely or otherwise related to the king did not yield to any officials except those officials exercising their functions. Thus, we clearly see the distinction between a political and administrative order on the one hand and a social order on the other. However, all members of the high nobility, namely chevaliers, had to give way to officials who were chevaliers by virtue of their office and did so even when they were outside the sphere of their functions (namely those of Chancellor of France, senior presiding judges of the sovereign courts, presidents, King's procurators, King's advocates at the Paris Parlement). And all ordinary gentlemen had to give way to all magistrates even commoners, in their area of competence, even outside the sphere of their functions.[34]

Loyseau attacks the gentry's claims to family superiority and purity of blood which represented insurmountable obstacles to the aspirations of men of the robe:

'The reasonable soul of men springing directly from God who created it on purpose when He sent it into the human body is not at all naturally connected to the qualities of procreation in the body in which it is implanted. That is why I am surprised that almost all the most esteemed thinkers and poets . . . have furthered the belief that there are certain hidden virtuous principles that are passed by birth from father to son, as witness the inductive arguments of Socrates who concluded that just as the bountiful apple, the generous wine and the thoroughbred horse were the best, so it was with a man of the noblest family.'

In addition, Aristotle, in the eighth chapter of Book 3 of his *Politics* says that 'among all nations, the nobility is honoured and esteemed because it is likely that a man has excellence if his parents are excellent and therefore he defines nobility as . . . family quality'. Loyseau disputes the validity of this theory:

'... And so one quite often sees children of upright men who are quite worthless and those of learned men who are quite ignorant ... and if at times children's characters happen to conform to those of their parents, this is not a result of descent which plays no part in character, but rather of education and upbringing where, indeed, children of men of quality have many advantages, and because of the careful instruction given them as well as through continual and productive example offered by their fathers and the commitment they have not to bring about the degeneration and downfall of their race. Finally they have advantage of the trust and good reputation created by the memory of their ancestors.'[35]

Thus, everything depends on education, good example and on one's heritage, not on one's blood-line. Everything depends on what a man can acquire for his children, not on those things that cannot be acquired.

Lastly, Loyseau uses in support of the men of the robe the old myth explaining French society in terms of conquests. The origins of the social stratification of France lie in the conquest of the country by the Franks. The victorious Franks were the nobility and the conquered Gauls the commoners. The Franks brought the Gauls into subjection, 'but they reserved for themselves the privilege of holding public offices, using arms and benefiting from fiefs without being liable to pay taxes either to lords of a particular place or to the sovereign for the necessities of the state. In return, they were only committed to fighting wars'. The conquered Gauls remained thus unable to hold public offices, bear arms, and hold fiefs and were forced to pay rents to lords of manors as well as taxes to meet the necessities of the state. In time, the two nations mingled, the Gauls obtaining franchises and concessions from the Franks and, with them, forming the gentry which retained the conquerors' privileges.

Gaulish commoners ceased to be barred completely from holding offices and fiefs or bearing arms. However, they continued to be excluded from the leading offices of the Crown and the Royal Household, governorships, military regiments, leading fiefs and manors, and remained liable to pay the free-fief for ordinary fiefs.[36]

Loyseau does not think of repudiating this myth because it was for him, as for his contemporaries, history itself. Yet he does not draw from it the usual conclusion, namely that the social stratification of France was just and reasonable because it was derived from the right of conquest. He draws quite a different conclusion, namely that the nobility is born of 'a public and general law', that it stems from 'common law', that it comes not 'from the law of nature, like liberty, but from ancient law and the state's disposition'.[37] One can see what this observation suggests. What is a law of nature is unchangeable whereas what is a law of the state can be modified. Thus, if one law of the state elevates a warrior to the nobility, yet another law of the state can elevate a magistrate to the nobility, not merely on a par with the warrior but even above him. A small change, made by the state at society's instigation, could in a given order-based society with given forms of nobility, make the magistrate the nobleman par excellence in place of the warrior.

The gentlemen fought against this tendency on the part of the men of the robe. They called the noblemen by office and function 'bourgeois'. So the historian can do likewise while specifying what he is talking about. What is this 'bourgeoisie'? The words 'bourgeois' and 'bourgeoisie' have a few different meanings. They can stand for 'the collection of people who inhabit a town', the townsfolk as opposed to countryfolk. Or they can mean the members of the third estate as distinct from the gentry and the ecclesiastics. Or again the epithet 'bourgeois' can signify a person employing workmen.[38] It can be simply a legal title standing for anyone living in a town, liable to meet a share of its financial responsibilities, belonging to the militia and who has been recognised as a bourgeois by the town corporation. Used in this sense, a humble shoemaker can be a 'bourgeois of a given place'. In certain towns, it was, furthermore, necessary to fulfil certain conditions regarding fortune, income and dwelling place. Principal masters of craft guilds and merchants can even be considered the only true bourgeoisie. But there is one meaning common among authors of histories of towns in the sixteenth and seventeenth centuries and one which is especially worthy of note: the bourgeois is the commoner, the town dweller who lives nobly off his *rentes* without carrying on any craft or trade and who, furthermore, has the right to the title of 'bourgeois of such and such a town', sharing in its honours and privileges, with a vote in its assemblies and possibly the opportunity of becoming a municipal magistrate. This type of bourgeois is certainly not a member of a social group of capitalist businessmen involved in producing material goods. It is likely that the noblemen used the term 'bourgeois' in this last sense of the word. At any rate, the terms 'bourgeois' and 'bourgeoisie' used in scorn when spoken or written by gentlemen do not take us outside an order-based society. However, this variety of meanings, so different from the one that prevailed in the nineteenth century, suggests that, whenever we come across these terms in a text, we look closely at the context in order to ascertain precisely which social group is being referred to. This particular precaution is not taken often enough by certain historians.

We cannot really call this a 'feudal' society although fiefs and feudal dues are plentiful and play an important role in the structure of society. It is indeed possible that this role was developed still further during the great economic recession in the seventeenth century. However, we are no longer dealing with the type of society that existed from around 850 to 1250 between the Loire and Meuse regions, which was a feudal society in the proper sense of the word.[39] We have instead a society in which fief and feudal contracts no longer dominate social relations. These are, instead, dominated by a hierarchy of ranks and fealties. Fealties have no legal sanction which is why official documents do not mention them and why one can so easily underestimate their importance. Within the order of the nobility, just as we find between the third estate and the nobility, men offer themselves to a 'protector', as a patron, and becomes his 'faithfuls' (fidèles), his *créatures*. They give themselves to him and vow their total allegiance, their absolute devotion to him and dedicate their services to him, fight for him in duels, brawls and pitched battles, talk, write and intrigue for him, follow him in his misfortunes, even abroad to far-off places, serve prison sentences for him and kill for him. In exchange, the master, or 'protector' provides food and clothing for them, places trust and confidence in them, ensures their worldy advancement, arranges their marriages, gets appointments for them, protects them, arranges for them to get out of prison and, if he is a prince, makes stipulations in their favour in treaties negotiated with the king to bring revolts to an end. The king himself can only have his orders obeyed through 'faithfuls' like these acting as intermediaries. These are the king's 'men' who in turn have their own 'faithfuls', their own *créatures*. Thus Louis XIII had Richelieu while Richelieu had Séguier, Bouthillier, Sublet de Noyers who in turn had their 'faithfuls'. The faithful does not become associated with his master by an act of faith and homage nor does he expect in return a fief in order to support himself. So this is not feudalism. There is, however, no doubt that these 'fealties' derived from the age of feudalism and the period of vassalage which preceded it. But one should not confuse the nature of a social system with its origins. Fealties are not linked to feudalism. They have existed in societies which did not know, and had never known, a feudal regime. They are something quite different and are characteristic of a different kind of society, at least another species of the great genus of societies of orders.[40]

What part is played therefore by the fief and the feudal due in a society of ranks and fealties? Probably they were, above all, a social symbol. Fiefs and feudal dues seem to have brought in relatively little to the 'direct lord', in several provinces at least. They seem in any case to be an unprofitable form of ownership. Probably, possessing a fief was above all a matter of rank and prestige in order-based societies because of sentimental attachment to these relics of the past.[41]

Notes to Chapter Six

1. Charles Loyseau, *Cinq Livres du droit des offices, suivis du livre des Seigneuries et de celui des Ordres*, Paris 1610. I have used the edition of Loyseau's *Oeuvres complètes* of 1678 prepared by Sébastien Cramoisy. References from this edition correspond to the Lyons edition, 1701, British Museum fol. 20.10 See Roland Mousnier, La participation des gouvernés aux activités des gouvernants dans la France du XVIIe et du XVIIIe siècles, *Recueils de la Société Jean Bodin*, tome XXIV, 'gouvernants', Troisième partie, Editions de la Librarie Encyclopédique, Brussels, 1966, pp. 235–99.
   Roland Mousnier, 'Les concepts d'Ordres, d'"Etats", de "fidelité" et de "Monarchie absolue" en France de la fin du quinzième à la fin du XVIIIe siècle', *Revue historique*, 1972, 2e fasc.
   Roland Mousnier 'Le tournant des Ordres aux classes', *Revue d'Histoire économique et sociale*, 1972, 1er fasc.
2. *Ordres*, Ch. I, p. 3.
3. *Ibid.*, III, p. 2.
4. *Ibid.*, IV, pp. 27, 28
5. *Ibid.*, VIII, p. 5.
6. *Ibid.*, II, p. 39; III, p. 5.
7. *Ibid.*, III, pp. 6, 7, 8.
8. *Ibid.*, Ch. VII.
9. Not 'knight' but generic title of the upper nobility.
10. *Ibid.*, Ch. VI.
11. *Ibid.*, Ch. V.
12. *Ibid.*, Ch. IV, p. 27; VIII, p. 6. Roland Mousnier, *L'assassinat d'Henri IV*, Paris, Gallimard, 1964, III: 'Les états généraux de 1614–1615'.
13. *Ibid.*, Ch. VIII.
14. *Ibid.*, XI, pp. 10–11, 27–29, 37–38.

15. *Ibid.*, I, 26–39.
16. Regiments attached to the King founded by Charles VII in the fifteenth century. Cf. R. Doucet, *Les Institutions de la France au XVIe siècle*, Paris, 1948, vol. II. pp. 620 ff.
17. *Ibid.*, I, 40.
18. *Ibid.*, V, 71–87.
19. *Ibid.*, V, 102.
20. *Ibid.*, IV, 44.
21. *Ibid.*, V, 38–48. L-N-H Chérin, *Abrégé chronologique sur la noblesse*, 1788, pp. 139, 140. Francois Bluche and Pierre Durye, L'anoblissement par charges avant 1789, *Les Cahiers nobles*, 23, 24, 1962 (with bibliography).
22. *Ibid.*, Ch. VIII.
23. *Ibid.*, IX, pp. 26–55.
24. *Ibid.*, Ch. V, pp. 88–110.
25. Roland Mousnier, *La vénalité des offices sous Henri IV et Louis XIII*, Rouen, Maugard, 1945, p. 501–6.
26. Charles Sorel, *Histoire comique de Francion*, I, p. 158.
27. *Lettres familières de Balzac à M. Chapelain*, Amsterdam, Elzevier, 1661, Lettre XXX, pp. 55–6.
28. Choisy, *Mémoires*, 2nd ed., Michaud-Poujoulat, p. 554.
29. *Journal de l'Assemblée de la Noblesse*, S.L.N.D. Bib. Nat. LB 37–1858, p. 79.
30. Roland Mousnier, *La venalité des offices*, op. cit. Book III, Ch. IV, pp. 569–587. Roland Mousnier, *L'assassinat d'Henri IV : le problème du tyrannicide et l'affermissement de la monarchie absolue*, Paris, Gallimard, 1964, III, Ch. III : 'Les états généraux de 1614–1615'.
31. E. Griselle, État de la France, de 1642 *Formulaire de letteres . . . et Etat de la France*, Paris, 1919, p. 245.
32. Roland Mousnier, *Lettres et mémoires adressés au chancelier Séguier (1633–1649)*, Presses Universitaires de France, 1964, I, pp. 169–70.
33. Here it is a matter of the king's officials residing in the towns, the *lieutenants généraux de baillages* and the *lieutenants particuliers* for example as opposed to the provincial governors, and not municipal magistrates.
34. *Ordres*, 'Avant-Propos' pp. 6–7.
35. *Ibid.*, I, pp. 33–5.
36. *Ibid.*, IV, pp. 1–3.
37. *Ibid.*, IV, pp. 28–34.
38. *Ibid.*, IV, pp. 38–40.
39. Roland Mousnier, 'Recherches sur les soulèvements populaires en France sous la Fronde' in the *Revue d'histoire moderne et contemporaire*, IV, 1958, pp. 107–8.
40. Vide documents in the author's *La venalité des offices*, op. cit., pp. 497–501. See also Orest's Ranum *Richelieu and the Councillors of Louis XIII*, Oxford, the Clarendon Press, 1963, J. Russell Major, 'The Crown and the aristocracy in Renaissance France', *The American Historical Review*, LXIX, 3, April 1964, pp. 631–45.
41. For a demonstration of this see the author's article 'L'évolution des institutions monarchiques en France et ses relations avec l'état social,' in *XIIIe siècle*, no 1.58–59, 1963, pp. 68–71.

Chapter Seven

The Administrative Order: Mandarin China

Under the Ming Dynasty from 1368 to 1644 as well as under the Ts'ings from 1644 to 1912, Chinese society was organised according to the traditional structures which it had preserved, broadly speaking, since the time of the Han Dynasty (221 B.C. to 220 A.D.). It was an order-based society, but it was organised not, as in France, on the principle that the profession of arms and the nobility of the warrior were supreme but on the superiority of a bureaucracy of magistrates, selected by competitive examination, holding total political power and deriving social rank and wealth from this power. Below the emperor, his family and a nobility of salaried dignitaries, were the three following orders: an elite made up of magistrates and holders of university degrees whose vocation it was to become magistrates; the people, the mass of the population whose life was spent in respectable occupations producing material goods—farmers, craftsmen and merchants; and lastly the 'wretched' persons whose life was spent in occupations that were considered base.

The social stratification of China had a philosophical justification, derived in this land-oriented, agrarian society from the contemplation of nature over which the Chinese had little control. Thus, the natural elements and their movements needed close observation and men had to become part of the natural order of things and be carried along by it. From this was created a special kind of cosmology which inspired a political philosophy.

The universe was conceived of as a succession of periodic, cyclic phenomena, forever repeating, with all things and all beings in it bound by a fundamental unity such that if one or other went outside the established order it brought about the disruption of everything else. It was a form of atheism because the Supreme Being Tai Chi whose action sustains the whole of nature, was certainly eternal and immaterial but, at the same time, without intelligence and will. However in everyday life, many Chinese treated Tai Chi as a personal and compassionate God, rewarding virtue and punishing evil. The fundamental political problem was therefore that of keeping the people in harmony with the universe's order of things. According to the jurists who had formulated their political theories during the era of the warring states which were finally unified by the Hia and Han dynasties, human beings all have the same basic needs. Though these needs are many, goods for consumption are few, so men quarrel and compete for them, bringing about distresses. Goods are too scarce to make equality possible, so hierarchical ranks have to be created. The more virtuous a man is, the higher his rank should be. The higher his rank, the higher his salary. This social order may be ensured by a uniform and equal law for everyone which a whole system of rewards and punishments will compel everyone to observe, be he ruler, minister, nobleman or peasant. Punishment must be severe and implacable.

The Confucians, disciples of the last 'Holy Man', Confucius (551–479 B.C.), increased their influence during the Han Dynasty. Although they integrated within their doctrines the jurists' basic concepts, they refined and extended them. Inequality is a law of nature, and the division of social labour, a source of inequality, is a basic condition of every social order. Men with intellectual gifts are scholars and magistrates whose function is to study, acquire virtue and to govern. They are the 'big men' with the highest salaries and the highest standard of living. Those whose talent lies in manual work are the 'little men' whose function is to serve and support the 'big men'.

Maintaining the social order, however, does not only depend on the law. It is also the particular purpose of Li, the social conventions, the collection of rules of conduct expressed in rites and ceremony. It is by Li that the reciprocal behaviour of people of different social levels is regularised. To gain respect for the social proprieties one must refine one's sensibilities through education. The minds of the people must be turned in the right direction by governing them with virtue, good example and persuasion. However, education must be assisted by law which has the power to enforce respect for the social proprieties.

Only differences in intellectual capabilities should differentiate men who should all have the same educational opportunities. The social order is based not on birth but on merit both of mind and heart.

During the Ming and Ts'ing eras, these ideas not only dominated the minds of magistrates and scholars but of all the Chinese people right down to the humblest peasant.

At the top of society was the head of state, an emperor whose position was a hereditary one within a dynasty. However, since only the best and wisest man should govern, the emperor chose the most able of his sons to succeed him regardless of primogeniture.

The emperor was an absolute ruler whose will was law. Yet he was not a despot. Indeed, he was not obeyed unless his rules harmonised with the directives of the sacred texts which were interpreted by the bureaucracy of magistrates. On the other hand, his power was only absolute in the political sphere and he did not attempt to govern the whole of people's everyday lives. A Chinese was free to choose his own trade, travel where he wished and buy and cultivate land quite freely.

In the eyes of the Chinese people, the imperial family had received a mandate from Heaven, the emperor being 'The Son of Heaven'. While he lived and ruled in accordance with the eternal Being and the natural order of things, his people were assured peace and prosperity. If, on the other hand, he ceased to be a man of virtue, nature became disrupted, with climatic disasters, epidemics, famine, war and defeat as the outcome. These reversals were all signs that the emperor had lost the mandate or 'divine commission' granted by Heaven. When this occurred, the Chinese people had to revolt and change their prince or his dynasty, a situation which occurred every 250 to 400 years according to a 'dynastic cycle'. Thus revolt, which brought the government back to the correct principles, was not a revolution as such but a part of the accepted order of things.

The imperial family was a very large one, with more than 100,000 members at the end of the Ming dynasty, though this was only 0.1 per cent of the total population. No imperial prince or member of his family could carry out any legal or administrative function. They were all simply salaried dignitaries crowning society and being, as it were, an adornment to it and models of excellence.

Below them came a hereditary nobility made up principally of soldiers, ex-soldiers and those related by marriage to the emperor. This nobility was made up of a hierarchy on nine levels, ranging in descending order, down from dukes, marquises, counts, viscounts who were on a par with magistrates of the first rank, barons who were equal to magistrates of the second rank and so on. Some noblemen were given military commands while some generals were given titles of nobility during their careers as soldiers. Usually, however, the noblemen carried out no functions and were, like princes, just salaried dignitaries and examples to the rest of society.

Next came social ranks that were not directly inheritable. One must put first among these, because of their importance in government, the eunuchs. Faced with an all-powerful bureaucracy, competitively selected, and with the strength derived from common ideas and traditions, even the ablest and most strong-willed of the emperors strove to find agents devoted to their interests and those of the imperial family, men who would keep them well informed and see that their orders were carried out. They found, for these purposes, eunuchs, who had been employed since the Han Dynasty. In 1644 there were 7,000 of them in the emperor's palace and 100,000 others spread throughout the empire. The emperor recruited them more than 3,000 at a time. Most of them had become eunuchs voluntarily in order to make their careers as such. They came from the ranks of impoverished peasants, vagabonds and the 'wretched ones'. They carried out their official functions in a specially organised group of twelve directorates, four offices and eight bureaus, in which they held grades corresponding to those of the bureaucracy. In actual fact, the emperor used them as councillors and commissioners, and they constituted both a political power and a factor influencing social mobility.

According to both the consensus of Chinese opinion and the law, the highest order in society was that of the civil magistrates and 'university' graduates from among whom this bureaucracy was recruited. Effectively, this was a competitively recruited bureaucracy, hierarchically structured and one in which promotion from one level to another was according to age and selection, but whose members had the powers of magistrates. Army officers, recruited through special examinations, were theoretically above the civilians but, because of the predominance of Confucianism, public opinion ranked magistrates above the military men.

This civilian and military bureaucracy had been given still more social prominence by the Ming. According to the *Annals* the emperor addressed for the first time in 1496, the bureaucrats and, in more general fashion, the graduates, as 'My Lords'. Only they were addressed in this way. The most cherished values in Chinese civilisation, desired most by the Chinese, were a post in the imperial bureaucracy, a long life and sons to ensure continuance of the cult of ancestors. Public offices brought with them the highest rank and social esteem together with the greatest wealth from the highest incomes in society. It sometimes happened, though, that a merchant or landed property owner was richer than a magistrate, but his rank and social status nonetheless remained inferior.

Civilian and military functionaries were drawn from among the scholars holding 'university' degrees. These degrees were awarded by competitive examination and, legally, these were open to all male Chinese. Society was receptive to talent and ability. The humblest peasant could aspire to the rank of minister and the Chinese were imbued with this principle. Reality, to a certain extent, conformed to this ideal. Studying was not an expensive business. One only needed to own the few basic classics, one or two history books and a few textbooks. Villages and patriarchal clans had elementary schools while there were free Confucian schools financed by the state in the chief town of every district and prefecture. It was customary for famous scholars and important officials to give public instruction in temples and public buildings as well as to open free private academies. Poor peasants, charcoal burners, brickmakers, masons and salt-workers came to these lessons and recited the classics. The government awarded scholarships to promising students. However, the sons of officials certainly prepared for tests at home with personal tutors, and, living and talking as they did with scholars as well as having sufficient leisure time, they were at an advantage in competitive examinations.

The graduates' vocation lay in public service though they did not automatically acquire posts as there were always far more graduates than positions available. One had to take one's turn, and, in this respect, the influence exerted by a father or uncle who had carved out a career in public office was invaluable. Magistrates' sons were at an advantage. The competition, however, did create certain ties and give rise to groups helping each other out, which was useful to those applicants who were without family influence to help them. The examiners became the patrons of those who passed the examinations and these in turn became their faithful followers. Holders of masters' and doctoral degrees awarded at the same examinations became, as it were, like relatives who helped each other out, however much their backgrounds might differ.

Rich merchants could, when governments were hard-pressed financially, buy the title of 'imperial student' without facing the examinations, and this would enable them to obtain a post or it even led directly to the post itself.

Graduating, at least at the third examination level, was like being received into a holy order. A man was something apart from and superior to the rest of society. The graduates were the head of the community. It was they who explained the proprieties and the laws and taught the people to follow the magistrates' instructions. And the magistrates had to consult the graduates who had free access to them without ceremony. While the common folk addressed the magistrates as 'Great Excellency' they had to address graduates as 'Excellency'. Graduates, like magistrates, had the right to wear buttons on their hats, in silver for those successful at the third examination, gold for masters and doctors, with the addition of a ruby and a pearl for a magistrate of the first rank. The colour yellow was exclusively for their use in their robes, as were the richest brocades and silks. They had precedence over common folk at festivals and ceremonies, in the street or on the roadways. Graduates 'could never be humiliated'.

Thus, if they were insulted or wounded, the offending party received seventy bamboo lashes whereas he would only have been given ten for insulting a peasant. Graduates could not be called as witnesses in a legal case by a commoner.

7

If a graduate was involved in a lawsuit he was not compelled to appear at the trial but could be represented by a servant. Special procedure was prescribed for graduates who, in any event, were exempt from being beaten with the bamboo rod. Graduates were exempt from all manual work and therefore from any services or chores for the state. Their property was subject to land tax, but they personally were exempt from taxation. Lastly, the lower ranks of graduates received from the government a salary, travel allowances and help in the event of famine. The graduates formed therefore a social order with distinctions and privileges. They must have accounted for approximately 0.25 per cent of the total population and, together with their families, 2 per cent of the total.

Under the last of the Ming, there were approximately 15,000 civil magistrates and about 100,000 army officers. Each magistrate retained all forms of authority himself. He was aided by clerks and copyists recruited from among those who had passed the first examination. After five years these members of his staff could take practical tests in a special examination, namely in writing a report or an administrative letter. The successful ones became magistrates though they were always confined to the lower grades.

Each magistrate had his orders carried out by 'runners' appointed from the wretched folk. They carried out the functions of bailiffs, messengers, police superintendents, jailers, archers, gatekeepers and policemen.

Each magistrate was surrounded by private secretaries. These were graduates who had undergone a practical training and constituted a kind of council or cabinet. They were also able to study for the higher examinations. The magistrate had recourse also to the advice and help of the local elite, namely those graduates who had not been able to get a post, retired magistrates and those on leave, such as those in mourning for three years after the death of a father.

Much of the elite's income came from remuneration for their services to the state and to society as a whole. Income from landed property formed only a very small part of their total income and, indeed, many members of the elite possessed no land at all or else very little. They were forbidden to engage in commerce, which was considered an unworthy occupation.

With the system of competitive examinations, there was a good deal of social mobility both upward and downward. Rarely could a family continue to hold important public offices for more than two or three generations. The elite was not a closed, hereditary group. Nearly a third of the magistrates came from families who had never had a graduate member for the past three generations.

Social esteem disobeyed the law and did not rank the peasants directly underneath the graduates, but the rich merchants instead. Merchants acquired huge fortunes from mining, the salt industry, trading in tea, foreign trade and in providing for the army. However, all these activities were state monopolies or under state control so the merchants played the part of auxiliaries in the public services. The state made commerce more a matter of administrative regulation than of production, taking all initiative out of the merchants' hands and not allowing them to compete freely. By virtue of services rendered to the state by their fathers, the children of salt and iron merchants were allowed to sit for examinations and competitions in any province they chose and a certain number of places were reserved for them.

In the country districts, after public service, land ownership—land being the chief medium for production—and the relationship of each individual to landed property, dominated the classification of the population into social strata. Chinese law divided land ownership into two levels; surface ownership and sub-soil ownership. The person owning both surface and sub-soil was the 'full' owner. If he owned only the sub-soil he was the absentee landlord, if the surface only he was the tenant. Absentee property owners were members of the elite and men of distinction who were commoners. From among the latter were also recruited big landowners who developed their property with the aid of farm workers and poor tenant farmers. Yet these big property owners remained excluded from the elite and the magistrates and graduates looked down on them.

Below the big landowners in the hierarchy of social strata came full landowning peasants who farmed the land with the help of members of their family and a varying number of farm workers outside their family. Then came a stratum of peasants who were partly full landowners, partly tenant farmers, some of them cultivating their land with the help of quite a large number of workers from outside their family. These constituted, within their stratum, a higher group of farmers, while others within the same stratum were helped only by members of their own family with, if needs be, the support of one or two servants. Then came those peasants who were simply tenant farmers, who, though some had large holdings, were for the most part cultivating a family-sized plot. Next were tenants whose holdings were inadequate to feed their family and who were obliged to hire their labour out to farmers or big landowners. One should doubtless place on the same level village craftsmen who, as often as not, were both farmers and tradesmen too. At the foot of this hierarchy which was perhaps an economic rather than a social one, were farm workers with no land or tools of their own, or money. The peasants formed a large social group, sub-divided into strata but each having its own customs and *mores*. Theirs was a precarious existence.

Lastly, right at the very bottom of the social scale came the strata of 'wretched people' engaged in the meanest occupations. They were treated as 'impure'. Their existence was explained by a social myth, namely that they were the descendants of criminals and unassimilated, conquered peoples. In actual fact, they were the outcome of a downward social mobility. However, they were trapped within their order with no chance of escape. They were forbidden to marry commoners or to buy public offices or university degrees. They received more severe punishment for the same crimes than commoners. Their 'impurity', their moral taint, coupled with the hereditary nature of this characteristic, made them a caste, the only one in Chinese society. The 'wretched people' comprised slaves, prostitutes of both sexes, singers, musicians, magistrates' 'runners', domestic servants, cooks, porters, labourers and odd-job men, boatmen, fishermen, oyster-gatherers, pearl-fishers, the social 'outcasts' convicted of theft or murder with degradation of their families and beggars. However, slaves could be liberated by their masters and, after three generations, their descendants were considered as commoners and were allowed to sit for competitive examinations. The 'wretched people' did not appear to represent more than 2 per cent of the population which seems a low figure.

Thus Chinese society was a typical order-based society.

Chapter Eight

The Theocratic Order

1. Pontifical Rome in the eighteenth century

All rank, honour and social esteem were awarded to the
Catholic clergy in Rome, at once the state capital and, more
importantly, the heart of the Catholic, or universal, religion.
Being an ecclesiastic devoted to serving the Lord Jesus Christ
was what qualified a man to hold temporal social functions
and offices, which in turn led to political and administrative
power and, as a result, large incomes and wealth. The
highest social order was made up of ecclesiastics and all the
other orders were arranged according to their relationships
with the ecclesiastics and the services they rendered them.
This was made all the easier to structure in what was a
relatively small town. In 1700 Rome had 149,477 inhabitants,
and 166,948 in 1794. 'In Rome people see one another and
get to know one another just like in a provincial town;
people know all about other people's business and there is
a good deal of gossip.'[1] This state of affairs favoured reciprocal social evaluation based on characteristics other than the
part played in the production of material goods or consumption capacity, other than capital or wealth.

The ecclesiastics who were at the top of the social hierarchy
were not the most numerous order. In 1719 there were in
Rome: 46 bishops, 2,622 priests, 3,652 monks, 1,097 nuns,
and in 1794, 49 bishops, 2,968 priests, 3,100 monks and 1,500
nuns. Yet they constituted the most highly regarded order
because spreading the Gospel and living a life in contemplation of the Holy Trinity were, at least amongst society's
conscious and declared values, those most highly esteemed.
The ecclesiastics enjoyed social prestige and, as a result,

were absolutely predominant in the state government and
the town's administration. This prestige was such that even
the laity often adopted ecclesiastical dress. This explains the
error made by a Judge de Brosses who wrote, 'Just imagine a
town where a quarter of the people are priests, another
quarter are statues, another hardly do any work, and the
last quarter do nothing whatsoever'.[2] The ecclesiastics had
filled everyone's mind with the idea that the highest form
of activity and the one most necessary for the good of mankind was their own, in its various forms; orisons, contemplation, spoken prayer, administering or receiving sacraments,
carrying out rites and ceremonies in God's honour. All the
rest was regarded as secondary or even despised, firstly the
military profession (and so much so that Roman noblemen
avoided carrying a sword and carried instead a cane), then,
above all, those jobs and professions that produced material
goods.

One had to be an ecclesiastic in order to succeed in an
administrative and political career. A prelate went from
'ordinary governorships' to 'general governorships' or
provincial governorships to get a nunciature. Doctors of
law could get 'ordinary governorships' but could only
advance further than this if they became prelates. Also it was
possible to purchase a vacant office in the Holy See, such as
Clerk of the Chamber, commissioner, or apostolic protono-
tary then acquire a bishopric and finally a cardinalship.
Whichever of these three paths one chose, however, the
overriding condition for reaching the highest posts, and thus
the highest honours and riches, was that one had to be an
ecclesiastic—belong, that is, to the clerical order.

The order of nobility thought of itself only as subordinate
to the clergy and as being at its service. Its principal function
was to help the ecclesiastical government of the State of
Rome by receiving foreign princes and rulers with excep-
tional pomp and ceremony, and to uphold pontifical

prestige with lavish receptions, banquets, balls and festivals. However, the nobility only existed at all thanks to the ecclesiastical order, and the aristocratic order was internally structured by degrees or estates according to its relationships with the ecclesiastics.

To become a nobleman, it was necessary to be descended from a family that was strongly represented in the high ecclesiastical functions, including having one relative as a member of the Holy College or, at least, holding high office in the prelature. This was also a necessary condition for being able to classify oneself as noble, and for acquiring and keeping high rank within the order. The highest stratum of the nobility was made up of princes and dukes 'who have rank, and do not live among the other nobles any more than if they were from another town'.[3] The second stratum of the noble order consisted of marquises, counts, barons and chevaliers, all of whom were wealthy. Then came a stratum of poor nobles with no influence because they had no relative in the higher echelons of the ecclesiastical hierarchy, the antiquity of the nobility, which was so highly prized in France, having virtually no importance in Rome. The noblemen assumed in their behaviour certain traits that were characteristic of the ecclesiastics in this baroque capital such as seriousness, formalism, pride, arrogance, contempt for everything that was not Roman, a taste for the grandiose, the luxurious, the magnificent and the ostentatious. They enjoyed privileges such as tax exemption or the possibility of trusts to avoid the sharing out of inherited property. They were the big landed property owners and land was the most highly esteemed possession. Yet this nobility had no interest in turning its wealth into capital and exploiting it on the market. They were quite content to allocate leases and rent out farms. The noblemen remained rentiers, especially seigniorial rentiers, with the wretched incomes this produced. They had no interest in industry for producing goods or in commerce for selling them. Their sole preoccupation was with acquiring governmental office through the influence they exerted as courtiers, manufacturing monopolies or monopolies in grain exporting so that they could dispose of them in return for ready cash.

The 'third estate' adopted the behaviour and sentiments of the clerical and noble orders; dignity, gravity, national pride, a conviction that they were the best Christians.

Below the nobility and above the 'third estate' came a kind of 'middle estate'. At the beginning of the century this social 'estate' broke down into two clearly defined strata. First there was the group of lay law graduates and clerks working at Court, in the offices of public administration and the law courts. Within this group came the *Curiali*, college bursars, comitial advocates, functionaries of the apostolic Chamber, the Capital administration and the Penitentiary, advocates and secretaries of the Fabric of Saint Peter, fiscal assistants, criminal and civil officials in the Treasury, in the apostolic Chamber, the Vicariate, the Tribunal of good government, the agricultural Tribunal etc. As a result the higher sector of the 'middle estate' consisted essentially of functionaries and employees serving the ecclesiastical order whose relative importance and social rank derived from the services it rendered this order and its relationships with it. Below them, the second stratum of the middle estate comprised public readers of the Sapienza, doctors of law and medicine, advocates and attorneys.

In the second half of the century, with Rome's economic development, a new estate came into being which was added to those above, namely a bourgeoisie in the modern sense of the term, and the expression 'middle classes' began to be used with the meaning it has nowadays. This bourgeoisie consisted of *mercanti di campagne*, or those farmers who had become adjudicators, the *camera apostolica*, who amassed considerable fortunes in this fiscal post and were able to turn them into capital by becoming businessmen trading in agricultural products and stock breeding. This bourgeoisie also comprised Roman bankers and a few industrialists in a society in which manufacturing remained technically backward. However, at the end of the century these businessmen grew richer, more numerous and more widely influential and were ranked with men at law and secretaries in government service. Thus, economic development at the end of the century changed the nature of the 'middle estate' which, while still an *order* at the beginning of the century because its importance rested on the social esteem accorded to those who served the ecclesiastics, had really become a social *class* at the end of the century because its members joined it by carrying out a role in the production of material goods.

The *popolo minuto* lived in squalid hovels often in the garrets of sumptuous palaces. Its members had a reputation for laziness and a taste for blissful idleness. They derived satisfaction from doing nothing or watching shows and entertainments with little concern for quality.[4] However, it should be pointed out that the highest stratum of this humble sector of the community was made up of very skilled craftsmen, all dependent on the ecclesiastical order as they were involved in all the trappings of liturgical ceremony, making reliquaries, chalices, ostensories, tabernacles, candelabra, candle wax, lavish costumes, as befits the magnificent religious services of the Baroque Age. Below them came the tradesmen needed to supply the town with foodstuffs, clothing and housing. There was not much industry in Rome and the town retained a rural character with kitchen-gardens, pasture-land and grazing animals right in the town centre. Nevertheless the needs of the inhabitants, travellers and pilgrims of all kinds, made for the existence of some 280 craft guilds, flanked by religious brotherhoods, and whose work was subject to very strict rules. All these craftsmen were certainly in no way lazy men.

Domestic servants were particularly numerous and had a reputation for arrogance and noisiness. Nonetheless their masters treated them considerately through fear of reprisals if they did not. It was customary for these domestic servants to solicit or demand tips incessantly and it was they who gave the town of Rome a bad reputation so far as foreigners were concerned.

Lastly, at the very bottom of the social scale, were a host of beggars, vagabonds, idlers and wastrels. They were sometimes drawn from pilgrims in distress who had come to the capital city of Christendom and had been unable to leave it, or from the poor of neighbouring provinces, other Italian states and sometimes farther afield, all of them drawn to this centre of Christianity by its reputation for charity. Indeed, in Rome, it was not shameful to be poor. Far from it, in fact, since the poor enjoyed special favour from the Church and charity had, moreover, brought about an extraordinary flowering of permanent institutions providing relief and assistance.

The whole of society was organised according to the principle of the social and political pre-eminence of those whose life was devoted to serving the Christian God. It was, therefore, well and truly a theocratic society.

2. *The Tibetan society of orders*

The supreme standard of value in Tibetan society was the Buddhist religion of the 'Great Wheel of Life'. Introduced very early on in Tibet, Buddhism was renewed by Atica during his voyage there in 1038. Since then, the search for Nirvanah by Buddhist contemplation has been considered in Tibet the chief aim in life, and monks, whose whole existence is devoted to contemplation, the most important human beings. External things, the evidence of one's senses, the use of reason itself and the truths that reason reveals, philosophy and science, all these are nothing more than illusion. Things that change, things that exist conditionally, have no reality. Things are 'like morning dew, like mist on a mirror, like the rainbow', just fleeting appearances. The only reality is the absolute, the only activity worthy of man is the search for the absolute and the only superior man is he who contemplates and can hope to attain the absolute. All monks, at least once during their lifetime, have to become hermits and be shut up in a dark cell for at least three years and three months, preferably nine years and nine months, in order to lose themselves utterly in contemplation. The behaviour of the laity is deeply imbued with monastic values. Anything that responds to the immediate appeal of the senses and instincts is scorned. Well-bred people do not admit of feeling hungry or thirsty. It is unseemly to say so. Thus, the monks whose life is devoted to a search for the absolute, are placed by social esteem at the very top of society and therefore of the government. When in 1253 the Mongol emperor Kublai Khan received Phagspa the nephew of the abbot of the great monastery at Sakya, Kublai Khan and Phagspa were on seats of equal height for discussing temporal matters, but Phagspa sat on a higher seat when talking of spiritual things, and Phagspa became the spiritual guide or national mentor of the emperor as well as the priest-king of Tibet, a rank which remained with his family as a hereditary title.

In Tibet, the monastic orders constitute the highest order in society, and political power is in the hands of a monk. The government's aim is to spread Buddhism. The role of the laity is to have children in order to perpetuate the existence of monks, to make sure that the monks can subsist and to meet the expense involved in religious ceremony. It is also to help the monks govern and administer Tibet. Every family, commoners included, provides at least one younger son to become a monk as well as the income from one field to support him. In noble families, the eldest son ensures the line of descent while the younger sons become monks. The Dalai Lama, sole master of all Tibetan lands, grants lands hereditarily to noble families but only on condition that those who receive an estate provide, generation by generation, a son to become a functionary. Those receiving two estates must provide two sons.

The ecclesiastical order comprised two main groups; the order of yellow monks and the different orders of red monks. The order of yellow monks came into being as a result of the reform made by Tsong-Kha-Pa (1360–1419). He forbade all magic, imposed celibacy on monks, proscribed fermented drinks and ordered monks to wear the colour yellow as prescribed by Buddha. The red monks were not reformed. It was the yellow monks who provided the Dalai Lama and the Panchen Lama. All the communities of monks lived in very large monasteries or lamaseries. Within their fortified walls was an agglomeration of large temples, libraries, shops, treasure houses, xylographic printing presses and monks' dwelling places, as each lama lived in a house with the disciple serving him, usually one of his nephews.

Monks came from every stratum of society. Only members of families engaged in base occupations like butchers, fishermen, smiths and funeral service employees; men afflicted with physical defects were unable to enter the ecclesiastical order. Monks were divided into ranks within a hierarchy. There were the candidates receiving instructions from a monk, usually their paternal uncle, then novices studying in a monastic college and sub-divided into several grades and ranks; next, monks proper, again with several grades and ranks and studying in the Tantric colleges. Because monks had to be self-sufficient and pay heavy dues in order to get into each grade, those who came from poor families rarely went farther than the novitiate. They carried out the functions of priests for the laity, stewards for monastic property, painters, calligraphers, printers, even carpenters, masons and tailors.

The monasteries derived their income from estates of which they were overlords, administering justice and raising taxes. Their peasants had to make payment of rents to them in kind, sometimes as much as a third of their crop, as well as dues. They were subject to *forismaritagium*[5] and had to pay a fine if they wished to leave the land. However since 1440 the lord of the manor no longer had the power to evict them provided they were paying their rents and performing their duties. The monasteries could engage in trade and commerce and they it was who sold to the inhabitants of their estates outside produce such as salt and tea. They indulged in a good deal of usury and granted loans either of grain or money. They received contributions and alms from noblemen and pilgrims as well as government subsidies.

The clergy formed a juridical order. Monks were exempt from taxes. They were also exempt from the state's justice, being subject only to the authority of their own order. Lastly, the yellow monks constituted the governing body in Tibet because their leader was the sovereign.

Monasteries had their own form of government and administration by monks who were classified according to a strict hierarchical structure. In the orders, high administrative posts in lesser monasteries were filled by graduates from the central monasteries. But abbots of monasteries were appointed in two different ways. In the old orders, the abbot was usually a hereditary official from a noble family, the post passing from uncle to nephew. The custom among the yellow monks was for qualified monks to declare that such and such a child from such and such a family was the reincarnation of the deceased abbot and should succeed him as the 'living Buddha'. All yellow monks could lay claim to a reincarnation. The Tibetans had four distinct ranks of 'living Buddhas': the Dalai Lama and the Panchen Lama; the four abbots of four monasteries at Lhasa; all 'royal incarnations' that provided a regent during the Dalai Lama's absence or before he came of age; fifty to sixty 'living Buddhas' who were abbots of various 'yellow' monasteries; and lastly lesser reincarnations, of which there were one or two in each monastery.

In 1697 the monastery at Sera near Lhasa had 2,850 monks. In 1663 there would have been in Tibet some 1,800 monasteries, with 100,000 monks, of which 750 were 'yellow' monasteries housing 51,000 monks. Around 1700, there would have been about 3,150 monasteries and 302,000 monks subordinate to the Dalai Lama.

The head of state and of government had been the supreme abbot of the Order of Yellow Monks, from reincarnation to reincarnation, since 1475. In 1580 the Mongol prince of the Ordos, converted by the abbot Sod Nam Gya Tso, conferred on the latter and his successors the title of 'Dalai Lama' or 'Ocean'. Thus we have, successively, the 'Ocean of Merit', the 'Ocean of Virtue' etc. The fifth Dalai Lama Ngagwang Lobsang Gyamtso (1617–1680) was in 1642 given power over the whole of Tibet by the Mongols. He created the high position of Panchen Lama of the monastery of Tashilhunpo whose abbot had helped him. Abbot Lobsange Chökyi Gyaltsen (1570–1662) was declared the fourth Panchen Lama, by reincarnation, an incarnation of the god Amitabha. The Dalai Lama himself is an incarnation of Avalokitesvara, the ancestral god who brought to the first Tibetans the six types of grain. Avalokitesvara is the offspring of Amitabha, god of compassion and charity, before whom he pronounced his vow of Buddhisattava: 'Help all beings and especially help Tibet'.

The Dalai Lama wields absolute power. He governs both

the lay and ecclesiastical sectors. Ecclesiastical government is controlled exclusively by monks while the lay government is in the hands of both monks and laymen coupled with them.

Temporal affairs were controlled by a cabinet working close to the Dalai Lama consisting of four ministers, three laymen and one ecclesiastic all responsible to the Dalai Lama. Religious matters were looked after by a large secretariat of four monks. The ministry of Finance was directed by four financial secretaries all of whom were exclusively laymen. Other government departments had an equal number of monks and laymen including the War Ministry controlled by a monk and a layman. Altogether the central administration comprised 175 monks, 30 per cent of whom came from noble families, the others being commoners and 175 lay men, all from the nobility.

Fifty-three local districts were each headed by two functionaries, a monk and a layman, in whom all power was vested. Commissions made up of both monks and lay members travelled through the provinces.

Lay functionaries could be assigned indiscriminately to a civil or a military post but, because of the pre-eminence enjoyed by monks in Tibetan society, the nobility held in lower esteem anything that was of a military character.

The lay nobles received instruction in a school of administration run by the Finance ministry, the monks in a specialised monastic college. The Dalai Lama nominated functionaries from among the students for a period of three years but the posts were renewable. Functionaries were classified into seven ranks. The first was that of the Dalai Lama; the second the regent, the 'living-Buddha' who held power while the Dalai Lama was coming of age, during his absence or between his death and the discovery of his reincarnation; the third rank was held by the four ministers etc. All functionaries were remunerated by being temporarily

8

granted land belonging to the Dalai Lama and they exercised the rights and powers of lords of the manor over the peasants.

Tibetan society was therefore well and truly a theocratic one.

Notes to Chapter Eight

1. J. de La Lande, *Voyage en Italie*, Yverdon, 1787, V, p. 20.
2. *Lettres familières sur l'Italie*, Paris, 1931, II, p. 5, no. XXVI.
3. Montesquieu, *Voyage en Italie* in *Oeuvres complètes*, Paris, 1950, II, p. 112.
4. J. Gorani, *Mémoires secrets et critiques des cours, des gouvernments, et des moeurs des principaux Etats d'Italie*, Paris, 1793, II, p. 144.
5. A fine paid to the lord if marriage was concluded with a person in another fief.

Chapter Nine

The Liturgical Order: the Muscovite state in the sixteenth and seventeenth centuries

By a 'liturgical society' we mean a society organised by the proprietor of the state for his own service, which is the service of the state. This definition enables us to distinguish liturgical societies from all those which have a social stratum or several strata dedicated to the service of the state; societies in which social stratification is spontaneous, although the action of the state influences it or else if the state organises society, where it is for the sake of society and the common weal and not for the sake of the state.

As our example of a liturgical society we shall take Russia at the end of the sixteenth and during the seventeenth centuries.

The head of the Muscovite state was the tsar. He was regarded as the hereditary proprietor of the state. Muscovy was his private domain, his *otchina*, hereditary within his family. Thus it was natural that he should have the absolute power of the proprietor over the land and over all the people that lived on it. This was a fundamental characteristic of the tsar's role. However, in addition, since 1472 when Ivan III had married Sophia Paleologus, the niece of the last emperor of Byzantium, the idea had spread that he was 'Caesar', 'Czar', the successor of the Byzantine emperors, who in turn succeeded the Roman emperors. He was therefore an 'autocrat' deriving strength only from himself, absolutely independent of and superior to any other mortal being, be he prince or king. Everyone was imbued with these ideas. The Russians revered autocracy and regarded the will of the prince as the will of God.

The tsar, as proprietor of the state, on principle organised Russian society and arranged it into a hierarchical structure in such a way as to serve him, and thereby serve the state. Russian society did not have, and probably never had, a feudal hierarchy. It had only the domain in which the proprietor wielded the power of overlord. Servants of the Russian state were remunerated by being temporarily granted land cultivated by peasants. But there was no such thing as the act of fealty and homage nor the hierarchy of overlords and vassals which was at the heart of the feudal system. Secondly, Russian society had no 'intermediate bodies' such as provincial estates, corporations, colleges, companies, even craft guilds. Corporative organisations were unknown. Thirdly, although state servants were primarily soldiers, Russian society was not dominated by the military and knightly ideal. No organising principle welled up from within society itself besides service to the state.

On principle, in the Russian state, a service state, 'the activities and obligations of all subjects, from the mightiest lord to the humblest peasant were determined by the state, in the pursuit of its own interests and policies.'[1] The tsar placed on his subjects obligations towards the state according to their callings and gave each of them certain special functions aimed at preserving and increasing the state's power and authority. Thus he divided social groups not into corporations but into service rankings or *chini*. The greatest lords were concerned with government functions, the lesser ones with the army and the administration. Wealthy merchants were assigned to collect taxes and carry on the tsar's personal trade while the peasants had to be tied to their lords in order to provide them with the material means with which to carry out their service towards the state. The aim was to fix society in a stratification of service rankings, structured hierarchically according to how important they were to the tsar, the state's proprietor. If the tsar granted a privilege or a liberty it was not because this resulted from an individual's right but because it was necessary for carrying out a particular function.

The 'servants of the state' constituted the highest order within Russian society. At the top of the order were the *knyazhata* or princes of the same royal blood as the tsar. They would have liked to wield power alongside the tsar and organise an aristocratic absolutism but the tsar never admitted them to his secret councils and imposed on them a written oath to serve him and his children, throughout their whole lives. Ivan the Terrible (Ivan IV) had decimated the *knyazhata*. After him there only remained a few of the old princely families, consumed with bitterness and hatred. After the 'Time of Troubles' (1604–1613) a small number of families, related to the Romanovs, still retained some prestige and influence but they gradually died out.

Below them came the boyars who had become noblemen by serving the Moscow prince. Most of them had become big landed property owners. Their rank in the official hierarchy was according to the length of service their family had given. The elite consisted of thirty-five families who had served ever since the first century of the principality's existence. Below these came those whose services had begun with Dimitri Donskoi (1362–1389). Lower still were those who had entered the service under Basil II (1425–1462) and among whom only two families had attained a position of eminence. All the families were recorded in the *myestnitchestvo* or 'order of ranks'. When candidates were to be appointed to a post, the tsar compared the ranks of their families together with the candidates' individual place in the lineage, and he chose the most senior one whose family had occupied the highest rank. It was from among the boyars that the tsar recruited the *Boyarskaya Duma*, a council which together with the Holy Synod formed the Council of the Tsar for matters of government and administration. The tsar also chose, in principle from among the boyars the heads of the ministerial offices or *prikazi*, his *voivodes* or military governors in frontier provinces, his commissioners carrying out all kinds of missions, and his ambassadors.

This hereditary nobility was decimated first by Ivan IV then by the 'Time of Troubles'. On the other hand many families died out naturally. The ranks of the boyars were thinning out. The tsar, in order to fill important state posts, to have councillors of the state, heads of ministerial departments and generals, had to call on either the medium-sized landowners or *votchinniks* as no one could be a landowner without being in the state's service, or among the 'state servants' who were remunerated by temporarily granted land, or *pomieschicks* of two or three generations standing, these forming a petty nobility or *dvoryane*, or again he called on even lesser men such as sons of priests, sons of peasants or butchers, who had distinguished themselves as soldiers. He awarded them titles, even made them princes. However these upstarts clashed with the ancient boyar families who continued to demand appointments and promotions according to the *myestnitchestvo*. They claimed that the tsar could grant anything except *otechesko* or ancestral dignity, in other words 'gentility'. They did all they possibly could to maintain their precedence. They fought pretentious upstarts in the middle of meetings of the *Bovarskaya Duma*. As a result of their complaints others were deprived of their rank, put in prison and knouted. Prince Pozharski who had been elevated from the rank of under-valet of the tsar to that of boyar and who had done much to deliver Muscovy from the Cossacks and the Poles, wanted to take precedence over Prince Saltikev but had to give way to him, was downgraded and forced to go to the Saltikev residence on foot and make obeisance. However, the insistent pressure of the new nobility and the need to replace extinct families gradually got the idea accepted that the tsar, by conferring a service of high rank was at the same time conferring 'gentility'. In 1682 the *myestnitchestvo* was abolished. It was the actual service of the tsar which conferred nobility.

Among the lesser 'servants of the state', the *votchinniks* and the *pomieschicks*, there were many graded ranks based on antiquity and 'illustriousness of race', on type and length of service, all this conditioning the extent of the *pomestya*.[2] Wealth depended both on birth and service to state. 'Servants of the state' were hereditarily obliged to do military service whence derived the obligation of civil and court service. Serving the state was a necessary condition of possessing landed property. The law of 7 February 1628 sanctioning current practices and ideas decreed once and for all that, apart from ecclesiastics, only those capable of serving the state could be landowners. All *votchinniks* had to serve the state or lose their property. The *pomestya* came nearer and nearer to the *votchina*.[3] Orphans less than fifteen years old and widows and their daughters kept a part of the *pomestya* until they were old enough to enter into service or until their marriage. The *pomestya* were bequeathed by will, given a dowry, handed over by donation hiding what was in fact a sale, or converted into *votchina*. In the end, in 1714, the tsar decreed that the *pomestya* and *votchina* were as one. All 'servants of the state' became definitively a hereditary, landed nobility, bound to serve the state and to supply a number of mounted and armed men in proportion to the peasant holdings on their land, personal allowances being deducted.

The 'servants of the State' formed three main 'estates': those holding office in the Duma, those holding office in a metropolitan town and those in office in ordinary towns. There were twenty-three magnates of Duma rank, only nine of whom came from ancient, princely families. All of them engaged freely in commerce and industry, enjoying the benefits of the large home market created by the needs of the army and the high degree of centralisation, and making use of the advantage they had of not being like merchants subject to taxes, tolls and customs duties on their products and being able to draw on the manual labour of serfs. Such a man was the 'grand boyar' Morozov whose power was based on his ownership of three hundred villages and hamlets in seventeen districts with tens of thousands of serfs. Thus, he could exploit potassium mines, iron foundries, leather factories, linen factories, distilleries, brick-works, flour-mills and fisheries. However, the majority of the country's needs as regards manufactured goods were met by craft workers or domestic industry whether peasant or seigniorial.

Below the order of 'servants of the state' came the order of 'town taxpayers'. There were many towns in Russia, all small, and excluding the capital itself, 15,000 inhabitants was the maximum population. Indeed, the majority of towns did not have a population of more than 1,000. Collectively the towns did not account for more than one twenty-fifth of the total population. They preserved a very rural character and their inhabitants were as much tillers of the soil as merchants or craftsmen. Towns were above all military and administrative centres with no true bourgeoisie. The town order comprised firstly merchants hierarchically arranged into three 'estates', 'best', 'middle' and 'junior'. The 'best' estate had to take it in turns to come to Moscow for one year in order to ensure that taxes were paid. Among the 'best' men certain groups stood out. At the top were the 'guests', a title granted to the thirty biggest merchants in Moscow who managed the personal home and export trade of the tsar, ran his iron and copper mines, cannon foundries, arms factories and glassworks. Below them came the 'hundred guests', consisting of 158 merchants. Then came the 'hundred drapers'. Members of these groups brought together a number of diverse enterprises and created a 'big' industry. The Stroganovs, former peasants, and owners of villages, employed 10,000 wage earners and 5,000 serfs in their salt mines, their potassium and iron mines, and the metal works along the Kama. They led the Russian incursion into Siberia and the trade in furs. But big operators like this remained a mere handful.

Towards the middle of the seventeenth century, merchants from every town were grouped together by the state into a kind of closed merchant commune, collectively responsible for paying their taxes and levies. Trade and commerce became a state-imposed obligation. Below the 'best' men the 'middle' and 'junior' groups, crippled with taxation and and forced loans, responsible for each other, and in competition with the 'servants of the state' who were exempt from taxes and dues when trading in their surplus goods, were often in difficult straits.

As regards rank, all 'servants of the state' were above merchants. If we consider wealth and income, however, 'servants of the state' in towns were all ranked below the 'best' merchants, and their different levels dovetailed in between the merchant ranks. Below the merchants but above the craftsmen came 'servants of the state of the lesser *chini*', that is craftsmen in the state's service such as smiths, carpenters, saddlers, gunsmiths, who, in their free time could practise their craft free from taxation. All 'servants of the state' moreover were at once traders, craftsmen and farmers,

Last of all came the different levels of ordinary artisans, all poor, living in hovels without chimneys, lacking tools. unproductive and earning very little money.

In the suburbs lived craftsmen, old soldiers, former peasants, priests' sons, or *zakladchiki*, or borrowers who gave a guarantee for their work. Their common feature was that they escaped taxation. The 1649 Code incorporated all these members of the population into the towns and made them liable to state taxes. Then the decree of 8 February 1658 made it a capital offence to leave one's town or get married in another town. Thus taxable goods and craft labour could no longer escape.

At the end of the sixteenth century the order of 'country taxpayers', the peasants, was far and away the biggest sector of the population in what was an agrarian economy. They were the chief source of taxes, provided most soldiers, and were indispensable in maintaining the 'servants of the state' both *votchinniks* and *pomieschicks*, but the big problem was to get them to remain on the soil when colonisation was opening great stretches of land on the Volga and its tributaries, towards the Ural River, Siberia. Peasants fell into several categories. On the land that was still directly owned by the tsar there were the 'black peasants'. It is said that at the end of the sixteenth century they were already practically tied to the land. On the estates of the lords, the *votchinniks*, *pomieschicks* or monasteries were the *krestiane* or tenant farmers who held the land in return for dues and services. Only they paid taxes. Below them on the social scale came the *bobyli* or landless peasants who were free agricultural workers. Below them were the vagabonds and casual labourers. Still lower came the *khabali* or peasants in debt who had given a lord an IOU or *khabala* for a loan of three to five roubles to be paid back by a predetermined date, and who paid interest on the loan by working on the lord's domain.

Legally speaking all these peasants were free men. The law afforded them protection. They could own property, go to law, buy, sell, enter into contracts and make wills.

Right at the very foot of the social ladder were slaves or *kholopi*. Lords used them as domestic servants, and as cultivators. Between nine and fifteen per cent of rural farm developments were cultivated by slaves.

The *krestiane* formed in every village a community or *mir* whose members were bound by mutual guarantee to pay state taxes. Their assembly elected and paid its representatives who in turn joined with the *votchinniks'* and *pomieschicks'* agents in that area or *volost*, in order to assess the taxes on members of the *mir* according to the nature and extent of their land, to collect rents and dues from holdings and to represent their district in dealings with the tsar's functionaries. Every head of the family reached agreement with the lord on the extent of his holding without having to refer to the *mir*. On principle the *krestiane* were free to leave their holdings and the community.

The *krestiane*, in return for their holdings, had to make payment in kind or in money (*obrok*), and services and labour (*barschina*). The lords, hard pressed by the weight of their service during protracted wars and the economic crises at the end of the century, became more demanding. They changed the *obrok* in kind to the *obrok* in money, thereby forcing the peasants to start trading and making things for sale in the towns. Some changed the *obrok* into the *barschina* and increased it from one day a week to two or three days in order to acquire produce they could sell.

The peasants, overwhelmed by this treatment, fled to new lands. The tsar needed their labour for *pomieschicks* and *votchinniks* so he sought to tie them to the soil. The *krestiane* had the right to leave their holdings and choose another lord for themselves on condition that they settled their dues and paid their lord to indemnify him for their leaving him. However, in the face of massive emigration of peasants, Ivan IV forbade, in 1580, all peasants to leave their present dwelling places without his permission. The 'forbidden years' followed each other at increasingly shorter intervals. As a result, in 1581 and 1592, registers were started in which the name of every adult male peasant was recorded together with his place of residence. A *ukase* in 1597 ordered all peasants who had fled during the previous five years to be sought out and returned to their lords along with their families and chattels. As for the *khabali*, by virtue of decrees issued in 1586 and 1597 they no longer had the right to discharge their debts. They were obliged to remain the peons of their creditors until the latter died. Up to then their creditors provided them with food and clothing and enjoyed totally the benefits of their labour.

In the seventeenth century, because it was necessary to ensure that 'servants of the state' had sufficient labour to cultivate their land, their chief means of support, and because there was a need to raise costly armies during long wars and periods of armed peace, it was essential in order to be assured of taxpayers and soldiers, to keep the 'country taxpayers' fixed in one spot. All the different categories of *krestiane* or tenants, of *bobyli* or landless wage-earning workers, of *khabali* or indebted peasants tended to fuse into a single category of serfs, bound to the soil. The indebtedness of peasants enabled lords to impose bondage contracts. The first of these seems to have appeared in 1628. Around 1630 they had become very numerous. But there is no doubt that state legislation and rulings were more effective. The 1649 Code confirmed a whole series of decisions taken earlier. Not only were heads of families bound to their dwelling place and fixed to the soil, but also all those living with him, sons, brothers and nephews. All prescriptive search for fugitives was abolished.

Henceforth the lord was the owner of his peasants, both of their bodies and their goods. He represented them before state courts except on charges of murder, theft and receiving stolen goods. He levied taxes on his serfs and made them over to the state. He had jurisdiction over his serfs for petty offences, brawls, drunkenness, larceny among serfs on the same seignory etc. He could administer corporal punishment to them. He had only to provide them with food and clothing. In 1678 only 10.4 per cent of peasant farm developments were cultivated by free peasants, 89.6 per cent being serf-cultivated. In 1680 the system was completed when slaves became subject to taxes and indistinguishable from serfs.

Left to itself and in peace-time conditions, Russian society would no doubt have evolved into a class-based society and, as such, an open society in which one's place in the social scale would have been determined by wealth acquired in the production of material goods. But the actions of the state and the exigencies of war made Russian society into an order-based society, a liturgical society that was structured into a hierarchy according to the services rendered to the proprietor of the state, the tsar.

Notes to Chapter Nine

1. Jérôme Blum, *Lord and Peasant in Russia*, p. 150, Princeton University Press, Princeton, 1961.
2. Land estates.
3. Patrimonial estates, as distinct from the *pomestya* estates granted temporarily for service and which gradually became hereditary.

Chapter Ten

The 'Philosophical' Order

The societies we shall be looking at in this chapter have never wholly been societies of orders. They lasted for too short a time for that to develop completely. However, in all of them, the first phase of order-based society, the fluid type of structure has shown itself. And, in the majority, the second phase of rigid order structure has begun to appear. These cases are all the more interesting because, while the Italian Fascists and German Naris fully intended to establish order-based societies—indeed the Nazis even reckoned on going so far as to create a society, made up of castes—the French and Soviet revolutionaries nurtured no conscious aim of substituting a society based on orders for the one they were intent on destroying and replacing by another, better one. Thus we will look briefly at the French Revolution up to 9th Thermidor, and especially at the French Republic of 1793 and the Revolutionary government. Next we will study Fascist Italy, followed by Germany under Hitler and, finally, Soviet Russia.

1. *During the French Revolution*

It is certain that not one of the revolutionaries wanted an order-based society. The aim of the third estate during the States-General of 1789, apparent from the outset when it assumed the name of 'communes' as well as the aim of the National Assembly from 17 June 1789 onwards was, on the contrary, to destroy the order-based society and establish a new one based on equal rights but unequal wealth and capital. In other words, a society made up of classes. 'Men are born to live in freedom and with equal rights'. The law

127

is the same for everyone. The professions and public positions are accessible to everyone regardless of family background and according to one's abilities. However, ability is not inseparable from upbringing and education which in turn partly depend on wealth, nor from connections that derive from social rank which stem above all from wealth, nor from the possibilities of expecting one's talents to bear fruit and from the economic means of bringing these talents into play, all of which depends on property, which is inviolable and sacred. The bourgeoisie had suppressed social orders. They also thought they had done away with classes because they threw open their ranks to everyone, at least in theory. In fact, though, the Constituent Assembly organised, and the Legislative Assembly endeavoured to make for the smooth functioning of, a class-based society. However, it is certain that the victorious bourgeois did not want a society of orders, of whatever kind.

The same was true of that 'coalition of socially disparate elements', the extreme republican 'sansculottes' where one finds a mixture of all sorts of people, craftsmen and journeymen, shopkeepers, minor peasants, some of whom owned workshops, shops and rural holdings. They were for equality in practice as well as by rights. They wanted, as completely as possible, equal distribution of wealth, statutory protection for and taxation of the small employer and his workmen, and of the small independent producer, involved in direct selling, as defence against the 'big men', the 'rich men', or big merchants and heads of large industrial enterprises, substantial farmers, bankers guilty of currency deals and joint-stock companies. They claimed the right to live, with the same conditions for everyone, the limiting of property-owning rights to what was earned by one's own work, workshop or shop, the right to public assistance, education, 'equality of pleasures', nationalisation of consumer goods, requisitioning of excessive possessions and free compulsory education. They pressed for the abolition of all social distinctions together with the utmost simplicity in everyday relationships, no airs and graces, no raising of hats, no 'monsieur', no impassive, authoritarian appearance, no 'lofty and proud' attitudes, no 'irony', no disdain of 'fraternising with republicans'. They wanted familiar forms of address (the informal *tu* in preference to *vous*), in all, a brotherly community of 'poor and virtuous' patriots. There is no doubt that they, like the bourgeois, did not want an order-based society with the hierarchical principle that this always entails.

Yet the revolutionaries had to fight for the Revolution's success, and in their struggle, they had to form associations, societies and parties. The behaviour of the Jacobins as well as that of members of popular societies suggested an order-structured society and, indeed, a society composed of orders might well have prevailed if the Jacobins or the popular associations had won the day and their power had lasted any length of time.

After the fall of the Bastille, political groupings had risen up on all sides to fill the vacuum created by the faltering government. Committees had been set up at the various town halls. Thousands of virtually independent local powers had taken the place of the now almost extinct central ruling body. For six months a great number of people busied themselves with community affairs, then the majority of them grew tired and returned to more personal matters when in December 1789 and January 1790 elections were held for mayors, municipal officers and provincial and district administrators. Temporary associations then broke up. As for the 'active' citizens and the 'electors' who had to elect officials of all kinds every four months, the majority of them, either grown tired or afraid, soon gave it up. Whether in the elections for municipal officials, or for 'electors' by primary assemblies of active citizens, or for deputies by secondary assemblies

9

of electors, abstentions were between 75 and 90 per cent. The majority resigned, leaving power in the hands of a minority.

The minority of 'pure' men, or those whose patriotism was the fiercest and who had the best understanding of the social contract, created political societies. The one which was to become the most important originated on 30 April 1789 when deputies from Brittany, the province of Dauphine and other provinces, came together and held, independently of sessions of the National Assembly, special secret meetings in order to co-ordinate their voting in a room in the Café Amaury at Versailles. The inception of the '*Club Breton*' (Breton only in name, incidentally) marked the beginning of the party, a new kind of pressure group, replacing the inter-mediate organisations found under the Ancien Régime. The 'Club Breton' only consisted of members of the National Assembly up to 6 October 1789. After the events of the 5th and 6th of October, having moved into Paris after the King and the Assembly and set up in the rue Saint-Honoré in the Bibliothèque des Jacobins, it admitted other persons of standing into its ranks which soon swelled to 1,000 people, 300 of whom were deputies. Its full title was the 'Society of Friends of the Constitution', but it was commonly known as the 'Jacobin Club'. According to its rules of association, 'the objectives of the Society are the discussion of matters that should be decided by the National Assembly . . . and the communication with other societies of the same kind that might be established in the kingdom'. The Jacobin Club gave rise to other similar societies. Following its example others arose in the provinces, one in Marseilles at the end of 1789, then in large towns. Federation Day was an excellent opportunity to indoctrinate sympathisers who took back to their small towns and villages rules of association and advice. All over the country similar societies were established on the same model with the same aims and with the same name. In June 1772 they numbered 1,200, almost as many as there were towns and enclosed villages; after 10 August, there were 26,000, almost as many as there were local parishes. The parent society in Paris provided them all with its rules, regulations and theories. It maintained a constant correspondence with them, published their official notices in its journal, endorsed their complaints, sent them watchwords that were usually followed, and tactical instructions usually carried out.

The Society of Jacobins exerted pressure on the Constituent Assembly, the Legislative Assembly and the Convention. A Jacobin deputy would move a motion in the Assembly which would get a hostile reception. Thereupon he would ask for this to be referred to committee and would get this accepted. According to their rules, the Paris Jacobins would then discuss his motion. They sent circulars asking their branches to do likewise and soon the motion was being discussed in 300–400 affiliated societies. A few weeks afterwards a hail of addresses descended on the Assembly asking for the motion to be converted into a decree and the Assembly then granted by a large majority what it had initially rejected.

The society of Jacobins indoctrinated the people. In a back room, when the Club was not in session, devoted members would instruct working men, explaining the constitution and acting as if it were a kind of permanent political university. The members of the provincial societies during their sessions, would read and comment on the Assembly's decrees, Marat's newspaper,[1] *Le Père Duchesne*,[2] *Les Révolutions de Paris*,[3] and sing revolutionary songs. If it was necessary to instigate a trend in opinion, a demonstration, a disturbance, a 'revolutionary day', the delegates of the Society, gathered in the Jacobin's back-room, recruited from the working folk ten agents who each transmitted the slogan to ten men belonging to various Paris battalions.[4] Through their agency, throughout every section of Paris and every battalion the same charge was made against the authorities, the same demonstration or riot slogan formulated. If needs be, the delegates might employ paid activists to train others. Similar or identical procedures were adopted by members of the provincial societies with respect to local administrations.

The Jacobins constituted a small minority. It is estimated that, in Paris at the end of 1792, out of approximately 160,000 voters, there were no more than 14,000 Jacobins. In Troyes there would have been between 400 and 500 out of 7,000 voters. In Toulouse the representative in charge had 300–400 men at his disposal. There were perhaps about fifty Jacobins in every small town, fifteen or sixteen in every large village, and five or six in every small one.

This small number of people wielded an overwhelming influence because they were inspired by an ardent belief in a doctrine which had for them a religious importance. The Jacobins were apostles of a new religion, the liberators of mankind. Their basic dogma was the sovereignty of the people, by which they meant not only the French people as a whole, the nation in its entirety, but each parish, district and, in each of these small units, the 'enlightened' and 'patriotic' segment of the population, a mere handful of men. The people have ownership of the Republic. They must be able to act themselves directly, form assemblies, deliberate, discuss control, have the right to put up public notices, to petition and to rebel. The people have the right to criticise the actions of their elected representatives, impose their own proposals on them, dismiss, arrest, judge and even execute them. They can ratify or quash the decisions of administrators, edicts or even laws passed by the National Assembly. The people are above all laws. In the name of natural law, they can break laws, edicts and decrees. They are above elected, regular and legal authorities who only hold power by their mandate and are almost their servants.

However, the real people are the Jacobins. Only they have knowledge of and will the social contract in its entirety, all the rights of man, liberty, equality of rights, and the sovereignty of the people. Only they know in advance what the most profound will of the people is and can act in conformity with it without consulting the other citizens. They can cogently show other people what they fundamentally want and dictate this to them. This will never be anything else than the revelations by the Jacobins of what the other citizens already have within themselves but which is obscure and hazy to them. The Jacobins can therefore impose a collective dictatorship with an easy conscience. Moreover their opponents are, according to them, violating the Rights of Man. Thus they are public wrongdoers, rogues, corrupt egotists, fanatics, aristocrats, enemies of the people who must be controlled or suppressed. In opposing them, the Jacobins held that any measures were permissible and acceptable, be this confiscation of property, imprisonment, deportation or execution by firing squad or guillotine. 'The Jacobins have every virtue. They are compassionate, humane and noble of spirit. But they reserve all these qualities for other patriots who are their brothers, something aristocrats can never be.'[5]

The party identified itself with its native land and patriotism with a spirit of sectarianism. The Jacobins' lofty idealism and extremism call to mind the Catholic Leaguers. 'Just realise that you are kings, indeed something more than kings. Do you not feel sovereignty circulating in your veins?' 'We shall be a race of gods.' 'Can a sansculotte be mortally wounded? Is he not as invulnerable as the gods whom he replaces on this earth?' The representative Baudot said, quite calmly, 'When Saint Just and I set fire to the batteries at Wissembourg,[6] people were most grateful to us, but in fact there was no special merit in our action because we knew perfectly well that the cannon balls could have no effect on us.'[7] These supernatural beings obviously embodied all truth, power and rectitude. All they did for the people was right and good. The end justified the means.

The Jacobin Clubs were therefore above all political and administrative authorities. They had lists of suspects circulated, made denunciations, conducted house searches, controlled local authorities, put up or withdrew candidates for elections, ensured that the vote went the right way. The Jacobin Club at Marseilles forced municipal officials to resign. The Club at Orléans wanted a seat on the High Court tribunal. The Caen branch burned the records of the proceedings against the people who had broken the statue of Louis XIV. At Coutances, the Club forbade its deputies to discuss decisions affecting the people. The Jacobins themselves were an arbitrary power.

However by the same token they set themselves up as privileged among the people. They were, in a great many cases, practically above the law, sacrosanct and inaccessible. Yet, in the same way, the apprehensive respect and consideration that surrounded them elevated them in society. As early as 1792 Mallet du Pan was demonstrating quite clearly in his paper the *Mercure de France* the growth of social mobility due to the shift in political power. The first effect of the Revolution was to substitute in the management of public affairs advocates for magistrates, bourgeois for ministers of state, ci-devant commoners for ci-devant noblemen, citizens for soldiers, soldiers for officers, officers for generals, priests for bishops, curates for priests, monks for curates, speculators for financiers, empiricists for administrators, journalists for publicists, speech-makers for legislators, poor people for rich.[8] Du Pan might have extended his analysis still more and shown a social order in the process of being formed.

In fact, the party was not based on only one social class. Jacobins came from every social class. The majority of them belonged either to the lower echelons of the bourgeoisie or to the higher strata of working men. Among them were lawyers, notaries, process-servers, doctors and small town surgeons, college professors, schoolteachers, journalists and priests. Slightly lower down the social scale there were bookkeepers and clerks, postmasters, master carpenters, non-commissioned officers, innkeepers, butchers, pedlars, grocers, tailors, shoemakers, wine merchants, hairdressers. What unified them all was not social class but their emotional involvement with a new form of religion. And all those involved were in the eyes of their fellow Jacobins something apart from and above the rest of the community, while for the rest of the community they were something apart and superior because of the fear they engendered as well as the success of their ideas. Within them were the seeds of a new society of orders. If they had been victorious, some time would have been needed for them to remodel French society according to their ideas. Inevitably they would have put themselves right at the top of the new social hierarchy which would have been organised according to the social esteem, status and rank merited by different degrees of intensity of faith in Jacobinism as demonstrated by one's deeds. A new order-based society could have been formed in this way and would later have become a society of orders of the rigid type.

The same thing can be said of the societies of 'sansculottes', the brotherhoods and popular local district societies that came into being around February 1790 and multiplied after 10 August 1792. Then when the Convention had suppressed on 9 September 1793 permanent assemblies of Parisian sections, there arose the 'sectional societies'. Doubtless all the members of these societies abhorred any form of order-based society but they too exercised political power. The Constituent Assembly had in September 1791 forbidden the popular societies to take part in political activity. However, on 6 June 1792 the patriotic society of the Pont-Neuf section decided to set up a controlling, watchdog organisation. From the beginning of 1793, the popular societies considered themselves to be on a patriotic crusade. They supported the Convention's governmental committee in order to get the Revolutionary government established and to further the war effort. They became affiliated with each other and with the Jacobins, but the 'sectional societies' became affiliated with each other without becoming affiliated with the Jacobins. They even tried, between August and October 1793, to federate into a central committee of popular societies. In the Parisian sections, between two sessions of general assemblies, it was the 'sectional societies' that ensured continuity, prepared projects and agendas for the general assemblies, drew up lists of candidates to be nominated for posts, kept watch on and control over officials and the production of materials of war, in fact held real power in their hands.

The sovereignty of the people was a dogma for the members of these societies but by 'people' was meant those coming together in the general assemblies the sections and the 'sectional societies' and exercising in these the whole of their rights. In fact, only the 'pure' minority could enjoy sovereignty, ensure the autonomy of each section, sanction laws, nominate, control and withdraw their 'elected' men, administer justice, impose their decisions by force of arms within the section itself, refuse to obey the administrators and the Convention, indeed rise up in rebellion—a right asserted moreover in Article 35 of the Declaration of June 1793. In short only they could carry on direct government by popular democracy.

Involuntarily the 'pure' men became a body of men separated from the population they were trying to involve. They were recruited according to the criterion of strength of belief in liberty, equality, sovereignty of the people and direct democracy. The conditions of entry were that one had to have shown proof of good citizenship and patriotism during the upheaval of the Revolution and to have been a man of action who had taken risks. A solemn oath followed by a kiss sealed their fraternal, mystical union with the other members of the society. They were all 'brothers and friends'. Their quest was for unity of faith, for thinking and acting 'as a body'.

They were, among themselves, all equal, but with other citizens they were separate and superior. They were the 'pure' men, the 'virtuous' ones. It was they who issued certificates of good citizenship, raised accusations of bad citizenship, drew up lists of suspects, separating sheep from goats, good from evil within the population at large. They it was who strove to involve all citizens in political life and appealed for resoluteness at meetings of the general assemblies. It was they who were suspicious of and who spurred on the apathetic, and tried to achieve a single-minded effort. They it was, too, who regarded it as a civic duty to control the actions, words and intentions of every citizen. They represented as it were, the leaven in the lump, the priests of a new religion, the outline of a new social order. The egalitarian organisation they dreamed of would have needed a constant protracted effort over twenty or thirty years to be imposed on the country. In this way their order would have been perpetuated and stabilised. Militants of a new generation would have had the support of their own children brought up according to their principles, and the order would gradually have become a hereditary one. Following its example and related to it, other subsidiary orders would have emerged in the country.

However, when the Revolutionary government was stabilized, the duality of powers—governmental and popular —became apparent as did, soon afterwards, their incompatibility. With the execution of the *hébertistes* and the disbanding of the revolutionary army (24–27 March 1794), the tide of revolution had begun to ebb. After 9th Thermidor (27 July 1794) sectional societies soon lost their influence like the Jacobins. On 25th Vendémiaire, Year 3 (16 October 1794), the Convention forbade clubs to affiliate among themselves and present collective petitions. On 21st Brumaire (11 November) the Club of the rue Saint-Honoré was closed and the Jacobins outlawed. After 12th Germinal (1 April 1795) and 1st Prairial (20 May) the sectional societies had to break up. It was the end of the 'sans-culottes'. A class-based society of a bourgeois type prevailed.

2. *Fascist Italy*

Fascism established itself in Italy in a class-based society and it did not last long enough to transform this society into one based wholly on orders. As a matter of fact, it was on 23 March 1919 that Benito Mussolini founded the *Fasci di Combattimento*. It was after a civil war lasting two years, on 30 October 1922 that the King of Italy made Mussolini head of the government and on 31 October that the Fascist columns entered Rome. And it was during the period 1925–1926 that the *fascitissime* laws marked the final triumph of Fascism. However, in 1935, Italian Fascism embarked on the Abyssinian war. In 1940 it attacked a France already beaten by the Nazis, joined in the Second World War and became nothing more than a war-time government. In 1944 Fascism was beaten. Its time for radically changing society had run out. Its enemies, moreover, charged it with having wanted to ensure bourgeois capitalist domination. But Fascists maintained that they were establishing a society of orders and their achievements led one to credit them with this intention.

Fascist activity preceded Fascist theories. In the beginning Fascism was a profound and sincere reaction by certain people against the great nineteenth-century movements of liberalism, socialism and marxism-leninism. It springs from deep within certain kinds of men as an instinctive reaction in the face of what are felt to be threats to all that one feels, loves, cherishes and respects, to one's very existence in fact, caused by ways of living and thinking that are repugnant and pernicious. Such an emotional reaction goes way beyond representing an economic situation. The ideas that spring from the action of these powerful feelings and emotions were developed and shaped by the Fascist theoreticians Alfredo Rocco (1925), Curzio Malaparte (1926), especially by Gentile (1923 and 1926) and lastly by Mussolini himself.

The Fascist Party engenders the state which in turn creates the nation. The Party 'is an order which one only enters to serve and obey' according to Mussolini. The condition for entry is faith, faith in one man, the chief or Duce, in his doctrine and in his mission in life. 'Fascism is, above all, a form of faith which has had its confessors' (Party Statutes, from the Introduction on 'Faith'). 'Mussoliniism is faith.' 'Mussolini is always right.' Fascism is a conceptual view of life, a moral law that binds individuals and different generations together in a single tradition and with a single mission to bring about a better life. It is a religious conception of life. 'It looks at man in the light of his sublime harmony with a higher law, with an objective will that transcends the individual as such and elevates him to the lofty rank of a conscious member of a spiritual society.'[9] The head of this society is God's instrument for creating a new world. 'Mussolini strides on with confidence, surrounded by a halo of legend, almost God's appointed one, tireless and infallible, the instrument of Providence in the creation of a new civilisation' (Gentile). The Fascist way of life is a struggle with oneself and with other men, through which the Fascist triumphs over nature and creates human existence. 'Our programme is "Fight" ', 'for us Fascists life is a continuous, ceaseless fight' (said Mussolini on the seventh anniversary of the foundation of the Fasces, 28 March 1926).

Only war concentrates all human energies most fully and leaves a stamp of nobility on the peoples who have the courage to face it. Therefore, Fascism is a spiritual movement inserted into a historical process. The Fascist must enter into the stream of reality and became master of the forces in action, and make his contribution towards creating history.

Fascism is therefore opposed to historical materialism because the Fascist believes in holiness, heroism and actions that have no economic motive whether direct or indirect. He denies that 'well-being brings happiness and that man ought to find happiness by being a sensual animal enjoying life'. Fascism is also opposed to democratic ideologies. Indeed inequality is necessary, fruitful and beneficent, and universal suffrage is a farce because sovereignty lies in other hidden forces. The spirit of egalitarianism leads to the disappearance of all high culture and discipline. Fascism rejects liberalism, another kind of materialism, because the liberal bows down to natural laws, allowing them to govern and lead him, cut off from other men and existing within himself, to a life of egotistical and fleeting pleasure. Fascism on the other hand is a philosophy based on the exercise of individual will, 'the antithesis of the whole world of the immortal principles of 1789'.[10]

The Fascist Party creates the state and becomes indistinguishable from it. It is established and governed by legal enactments. Its code and regulations are a public rule stemming officially from the head of state. They are laid down by decree at the proposal of the Duce who is both head of government and Party leader and on the recommendation of the Council of Ministers and the Great Council of Fascism. According to the rulings of the 17 November 1932, every large urban centre must have separate *fasces* for local defence, for young men, and for girls. All the *fasces* in a given province form a federation and in the chief town in the province is a university Fascist group.

The Party is arranged in a strict hierarchy and is rigorously centralised. Its leader is *il Duce*, Mussolini. It is he who proposes the Party's general secretary, who is appointed by royal decree. At the proposal of the secretary general, the head of government, the Duce, nominates the federal secretaries and the members of the national Directory. The Party's general secretary chooses the provincial federal directories, the secretaries and directories of local *fasces*. Everyone receives directives from the Great Council of Fascism under the overriding authority of the Duce. The directories have a mere consultative function. A disciplinary court and provincial disciplinary committee pass judgement on any lapses among Fascists such as disobedience, lessening of faith, flagging morale or lack of integrity.

The state is absorbed into the Party From 12 December 1926 onwards the bundles of sticks around the axe, carried by the Roman lictors, which had been the Party emblem, became the state's emblem also. The twenty-eight of October, the anniversary of the Fascist's March on Rome, was made a public holiday. The Duce, the Party leader, was head of government with the King of Italy remaining head of state. On 19 December 1926, the Party's general secretary became a high state dignitary and acquired special rank in public ceremonies. Public offices were monopolised by the Party and the law passed on 24 December 1925 set aside public duties and positions for its members. Provisionally, advocates of a 'wait-and-see' policy as well as those who were only lukewarm followers of Fascism were tolerated but all controlling positions were held by zealous Party members. At every level, Party leaders were automatically qualified to attend the meetings of councils and committees directly appointed by the government or by its local representatives. Lastly, the laws passed on 9 December 1928 and 14 December 1929 declared the Great Fascist Council an organ of the state and the national Fascist Party integrated within the

Constitution. Thus the whole state, the government and the administration in their entirety, came under the direction or control of the Party. In this Church-like body which was the State, a spiritual order was established in which the Party's mission was to educate and to spread the gospel of Fascism. It furthered the spread of Fascist doctrine and sustained the enthusiasm and fervour of the population at large. To this end, it made use of a whole host of Fascist associations, in the schools, in public service, the railways, sporting bodies, country households, and in the organising of leisure time activities etc. Party members have places in every administrative organisation where they are an essential element at every level. The general secretary of the Party is entitled to the rank of minister. He acts in liaison with the leaders of the House of Representatives and the Senate, the members of the senior Committee on National Defence and the national council of Public Corporation etc.

However, Party members became increasingly a privileged, closed and hereditary order within the country. Up to 1922, its membership was drawn from among anyone who wanted to belong, but from the march on Rome up to 1925 there was strict control over enrolments. From 1925 and the *fascitissime* laws, onwards, recruitment was principally made by selection among young people, the best of whom came suitably indoctrinated into the Party. Initially a child would belong to the *balilla*, from 8 to 14 years of age, the *balilla excursionisti* from 8 to 12 years, and the *balilla moschettieri*[11] from 12 to 14 years. He would then go through the *avanguardisti*, that is the *avanguardisti moschettieri*[11] (14 to 16 years) then the *avanguardisti mitraglieri*[12] (16 to 18 years). At eighteen years of age he joined the Party proper, receiving his membership card and militiaman's carbine, and taking the oath: 'In the name of God and Italy, I swear to carry out without question the Duce's orders and to serve with all my might and, if necessary, my blood, the cause of the Fascist revolution.' In fact, it was especially sons of Fascists that were admitted to the Party which became a hereditary order.

As may be imagined, this was a privileged order. All jobs connected with the state were primarily reserved for its members as were, in fact, all posts of responsibility. Sporting the Party's badge, carrying the lictor's bunch of rods and the emblem P.N.F. (*Partito Nazionale Fascista*) ensured that one got on in life. According to a legal provision made on 27 May 1932, during a period of unemployment, Party members received preferential treatment as regards the allocation of positions and jobs etc. At all times, Party members were preferentially treated even when it came to jobs in private organisations, if these posts called for social influence, and, generally speaking, they enjoyed priority over others in the whole business of getting employment. After conquering the state by force, the victors consolidated their position by forming an armed, hereditary aristocracy, the nation's highest order.

In 1933 the Fascist Party had some three million members, while youth organisations had two million.

The Party created its own state. Fascism was a form of state socialism, a 'statocracy'. The state is 'the individual's true form of reality'. 'The individual only exists as he does within the state, subordinate to the state's exigencies . . . as civilisation becomes more and more complex, the liberty of the individual gets progressively more restricted.' 'The state is the absolute value in the face of which individuals and groups are only relative. Individuals and groups are only conceivable as part of the state.' The state 'represents the people for negotiations'. 'Everything within the state, nothing against the state, nothing outside the state.'[13]

The Fascist state is a totalitarian one. Indeed,

'the Fascist state has a consciousness, a will . . . the state . . . is a spiritual and moral fact because it cements together the nation's political, legal and economic organisation, and this organisation is a manifestation of the spirit of the people. The state both protects and propagates this spirit . . . The state it is that represents the immanent conscience of the nation . . . that schools individuals in civic qualities, makes them conscious of their mission in life and unifies them.'[14]

As a result Fascism denies the nation's sovereignty and the free election of its government. The masses by themselves are incapable of having a will of their own, still less of choosing men to represent them by themselves. They allow themselves to be led by schemers. Moreover, the individual is nothing more than an instrument of the state.

Political representation is therefore something special in the Fascist system. Fascist trade union confederations put forward a number of candidates, effectively twice the number of parliamentary seats open for election, that is 800 candidates. The national committee of each confederation specifies its candidates by acclamation. Private associations of general interest, concerned with culture, education, relief work, academies, old soldiers' associations etc. put up 200 candidates. From the list of 1,000 names, the Great Council of Fascism would choose the parliamentary members. The electorate casts its vote on the following question: 'Do you approve of the list of members or not?' In order to be an elector, one had to be twenty-one years of age, or eighteen years old if already married with children, pay a union subscription or 100 lire in direct taxation or be salaried. In effect, deputies were already appointed. They were not representatives of the people but of the state, as all power resided in the state and parliament was an organ of the state.

Fascist government is a monocracy. It does not depend on houses of parliament, whether the lower house of elected representatives or the upper house or senate nominated for life by the king and embodying the permanent, solid interests of the nation. Effectively, only the sovereign and the head of the government can be judges and arbitrators of the situation at times of national importance because they alone embody all the nation's vital and effective forces. The government passes laws by decree and wields every aspect of executive power. It directs the organisation and day-to-day running of the state's administrative functions as well as the operation of public establishments and institutions. It approves the contracts drawn up by the state. It can even legislate either when a law of the land delegates this responsibility to it, directly, on a given issue, or on its own initiative in extraordinary circumstances when pressing reasons or absolute necessity demand it. The government has a direct influence on the legislative work of the assemblies as the prime minister and head of government, Mussolini, is in sole control of the business put before the lower house and he can ask for a rejected bill either to be transmitted to the upper house or put to a fresh vote three months later without preliminary discussion.

Parliamentary responsibility was suppressed. Under the law of 24 December 1926, the king holds executive power 'by means of his government'. The king reigns but does not govern. He has no responsibility. He chooses the head of the Fascist government in his capacity as leader of the Fascist Party, in other words, Mussolini, who as head of the government is in fact empowered in the king's name to nominate senators, dissolve the House of Representatives, close or prorogue parliamentary sessions, and to grant pardons or declare an amnesty. He proposes which ministers shall be appointed or dismissed, and what their duties shall be. It is also he who directs and co-ordinates their activities, convenes Council meetings and presides over them. Besides this, he personally directs the activities of ministers of his choosing, has effectively command of the army, navy, and the militia providing for the security of the state. He has under his personal and direct domination every large state body and presides over the twenty-two corporations and their national council. Furthermore, his person is sacred and inviolable. He presides over the Great Council of Fascism, chooses its members and allocates their duties to them, calls meetings and decides on the business it will discuss. But the Great Council is 'the regime's most important body' (according to the law of 9 December 1928), and its agenda were commands. All that remains, when it has issued its directives, is for the statutory machinery of king, council of ministers and Parliament to operate as intermediaries in giving them the appropriate legal framework. The Fascist form of government is an autocratic one.

The Fascist state creates and shapes the nation. 'Without the state, there is no nation, but only human aggregates, capable of undergoing all the buffetings that history can inflict on them.' 'The nation is created by the state which gives the people . . . a collective will, and consequently, an effective form of existence.'[15] The nation organised by the state takes a form close to the heart of order-based societies, the corporate one. To the Fascists, class struggles are pathological and should die out if everyone collaborates with everyone else in social groups that both unite and transcend social classes, namely corporations. In 1927 the Workers' Charter declared that 'Work is a social duty . . . the complex machinery of production is homogeneous from the national point of view . . . Its objectives are to develop the nation's strength . . .'. Therefore there are no longer any employers or employees, only producers. And in a speech made on 6 October 1934, Mussolini declared: 'The corporate solution is one in which the discipline of production is entrusted to industrial producers . . . , employers . . . but I also mean by the word "producers" the workers.'

In this respect the Fascist state claimed to be a state of the people because it broadened the recruitment of elites, facilitated social mobility and organised the conscious, lasting participation of the masses in the life of the state. This was different from the liberals and democrats who confused nation and people where nation is an indefinite string of successive generations, an ideal form of collectivity, unlimited quantitatively and temporally, and the people are nothing more than occasional aggregates produced by a fortuitous and temporary state of co-existence.

The corporative Fascist state claimed that it corresponded to the new economic and social conditions: professional groups, industrial and financial concentrations, urbanisation and the rapid communication of ideas all create fierce reactions in opinion. And so the Fascist state is itself the archetypal corporation. Its first function is a corporative one, namely to draw together into constant unity those individuals with a tendency to diverge from it. This is the supreme function of the state. Fascism was corporatism and therefore, essentially, union and unity. It thought it had found the best means of spreading, in the most rapid and most effective possible way, the will of the central authority into every sector of the corporate society and of putting at the disposal of the central authority all the vital forces within society through trade unions and corporate bodies, under the spiritual direction and sway of the *Partito Nazionale Fascista*.

At the same time the *Fasci di Combattimento* and, under their control, Fascist trade unions had been established with the title of corporations. In 1922 the Confederation of Fascist Trade Union Corporations that brought together employers and workers was centralised. The *Fasci*, the political element, appointed the men to control it. From 1923 to 1925 these corporations succeeded in monopolising working-class representation.

In 1926 laws were passed which declared the various corporations to be organs of the state, and set up a ministry of Corporations. Twenty-two corporations embracing the major production activities, namely cereals, vine-growing, metal works, clothing etc, gave those unions that had displayed 'good conduct from the nation's standpoint' and whose representatives satisfied 'the regime's political requirements', the title of 'recognised association'. Then, 'recognised associations' were given the status of public law personality and invested with power in public affairs, namely the monopoly over controlling working conditions; a monopoly on legal representation up to the level of the National Council of Corporations; and the right to levy a trade union subscription on everyone. In 1930 the National Council of Corporations was formed.

Strikes and lock-outs were forbidden. Public authorities could refuse to recognise the leaders of corporations and trades unions, could remove them from office, dissolve their governing councils, appoint a temporary leader, quash their decisions, and authorise important decisions beforehand.

The Charter of Labour of 1927 proclaimed the State an economic unit whose productive forces must be harmonised; authority must be reserved for employers, and as private ownership of the means of production was preserved, it has been possible to accuse Fascism of protecting the capitalist classes. The workers were to benefit from being active collaborators in the business and from collective work contracts enforced by the labour tribunals.

The trades unions became a public service, state-controlled bodies charged with administering the world of labour. The public authorities forced them to accept the leadership of professional syndicalists who were Fascists, trained at a special school in Pisa, and working their way up as in any other career.

On every Council of the Corporations, which were organs of the state, were three delegates from the Fascist party. The vice-president, who presided over the debates, was a Party member. The president of the Council was the minister who was a Party member of the secretary general of the Party. Mussolini appointed the members of the Councils of the Corporations. These councils constituted the economic structure of the state.

Thus the Fascist Party, after making sure of its power within the state, reorganised society on the principle of a social hierarchy based on attachment to the Party and services rendered to the Party. The shift from a class-based society to an order-based society was not completed through lack of time. But the intention to suppress class-based society and replace it by order-based society is very clear and undeniable.

3. *Nazi Germany*

The Germany over which Hitler took power was a markedly class-structured society. In this country of much industrial activity, with its monopolistic tendencies and big landed property owners, there were two dominant classes, the capitalist haute-bourgeoisie, the big property owners almost all of them squireens and junkers, dedicated to serving in the highest civil and military posts. Then came the middle classes, the tradespeople, small businessmen, clerks and functionaries, craftsmen together with an intelligentsia of professors, literary men, journalists, jurists, doctors and engineers. At the foot of the social ladder came first of all the workers whom the German Socialist Party (S.P.D.) had made into a quite separate class by giving them their own military corps to defend the Republic (*Reichsbanner*), their own clubs, co-operatives, choral societies, shooting clubs, mutual aid associations and, in many small industrial towns, most of the municipal functions. However, the class structure was undermined by the difficulties occasioned by defeat, the problem of war reparations and the world economic crisis in 1929. In almost every strata of society desperate young people, caught up in a situation of endless diplomas and titles and a derisory number of jobs in a world where one needed to have the equivalent of university entrance requirements to qualify for a job as a hairdresser's assistant or to measure lengths of cotton cloth, lived in a conquered country, in a civilisation in which a universe of algebraic concepts separated man from nature. They had nothing to look forward to but resignation, boredom and misery. Old soldiers were scarred by defeat, humiliation, inflation and ruins. The class-based society broke up of its own accord and the pieces were ready then to be refashioned into different combinations.

This is the society that Hitler wanted to change into a society made up of orders, then later, no doubt, of social castes. However, for him too, there was not enough time or leisure to bring this all about. He founded the National German Workers' Party on 7 January 1919 and in December 1920 this became the German National Socialist Workers' Party. He was slow in coming to power. On 30 January 1933, President Hindenburg appointed him Chancellor, or head of government. On 4 February, Hitler received full executive power then, after the Reichstag fire on 27 February, an edict abolished the fundamental rights that still limited his plenary powers and, on 24 March, he obtained complete legislative power. After Hindenburg's death on 2 August 1934, Hitler also carried out the functions of President. However from 1938 onwards, with the annexation of Austria, he began his grand military operations that would lead, in September 1939, to the Second World War, and in May 1945, to Hitler's death among the ruins of Berlin and Germany's surrender. It was a brief, crowded period of history in which to bring about the complete transformation of a whole society.

Hitler, nevertheless, set his hand to creating a new order-based society. He firmly applied a doctrine the broad outlines of which were already established in 1925 and which was published in two books, Hitler's own *Mein Kampf* ('My Struggle') which became the Bible of Nazism, taught in schools and made required reading for all officials, and Rosenberg's *The Myth of the Twentieth Century* whose author, in Hitler's judgement, had the most thorough understanding of Nazism. This book went through 142 editions before the Second World War. Subsequently Nazi theoreticians emphasised such and such a point and developed it as circumstances required.

As with Fascism, Hitlerism was characterised by actions before theories. It represents a response to events by proud, violent and domineering men carried along by powerful instincts who could not reconcile themselves to defeat, humiliation, inflation and chaos and who rebelled against everything that seemed to be the cause of all these, against the established order of things, democracy, liberalism, socialism, pacifism, internationalism and humanitarianism. But action gave rise to theory.

Hitler spoke of 'The eternal Being who is our Creator'. By this he meant a pantheistic God. The cosmos or universe exists as does a supreme Being, living, immense and mysterious—God. This living universal Being is manifest in various forms, in its emanations, its creations, in all things including man himself. These diverse forms are nature which is an aspect of God's being. The living universal Being is ever evolving into increasingly simple and perfect forms. God's will is therefore to raise the level of all beings and thereby improve Himself. God moves for all eternity towards perfection. Everything is in an eternal state of becoming which in itself is progress.

Living beings, including mankind, form different races. The human races are groups of men characterised by certain hereditary and unchangeable traits which are transmitted particularly by one's blood. Not only do physical characteristics derive from blood lineage but also intellectual and moral attributes, thoughts and feelings. Ideas are suggested to man by his blood. From the blood, for instance, come myths, tales that interpret nature in a biased and often vague way which are necessary to man who cannot do without them.

The hereditary and unchangeable characteristics of a given group of men do not belong to any other group, and, therefore, distinguish the different races one from another quite clearly. The human races are so different from each other that the lowliest of them is nearer to the highest species of animal than to the highest species of human being. The Jews are closer to the monkeys than to the Aryan German. The supreme race of human beings is the Aryan, the Greek, the Teuton, the creator of the whole of modern civilisation, its arts, sciences and technical achievements. The Aryan is naturally endowed with genius. As soon as he is put in the right climatic, geographical and social conditions and has subjugated foreigners of lower race who provide him with his slaves, in various forms, the Aryan develops the intellectual and organisational faculties lying dormant within him. Within the space of a few centuries or a few millennia, he creates a magnificent civilisation. All known civilisations, the Hindu, Greek, Germanic and French, were brought about by small groups of Aryans who conquered and led less gifted peoples.

God and Nature seek to raise the level of the races because God, who is manifested in all beings, and therefore in all races also, moves towards perfection. Raising the level of humanity can only be achieved by racial purity and by struggling for existence. In fact, crossing two beings of unequal value produces, as the offspring, an intermediate type and thus brings about decline. When Aryans begin to marry with their subject people, their children are inferior to them. As only the Aryan is capable of creation, the progress of the civilisation he has brought about slows up, comes to a halt. Then, if racial crossbreeding continues, the civilisation goes into a decline. 'The man who forgets and scorns the racial laws . . . impedes the triumphant march of the master race and thereby the necessary pre-condition for all human progress.' Crossing races is 'a sin against the will of the Eternal Creator' (according to Hitler). The struggle for existence brings about natural selection. 'Combat is always the means of building up health and resilience of a species, and, as a result, it is a necessary pre-condition for its progress.' In combat, only the strongest and healthiest survive and they in turn procreate and the race is improved. Increasing in numbers, the master race destroys inferior races by mass slaughter or represses them by deportation; it makes room for itself, increases in numbers still more, reduces the inferior races to the level of manual labourers, and never ceases to create. 'The man who wants to live must fight!' 'The law (of the world) is a constant struggle.'

The blood coursing through a man's veins is what gives him his racial spirit. Race, therefore, is above all other things the basic element that goes to make up a people (*Volk*) and give it a common spirit (*Volksgeist*). God is immanent in the *Volk*: 'The German *Volk* is the race chosen from among all others to educate humanity.' The racist laws in 1933 established as the foundation of the new German public law, racial unity and racial inequality. They declared the German people to be of pure Nordic Aryan stock, dismissed from public office and the professions of journalist and barrister, all those who were not pure Nordic Aryans. Because they kept a privileged place in society and state for the racially pure, these laws tended therefore to lay the foundations for a caste-based society.

However, too strict a racist formula presented one difficulty : it was obvious that pure Nordic-type Aryans constituted only a very tiny minority of the German people. The Nuremburg laws of 15 September 1935 therefore introduced distinctions. All peoples are the result of racial mixing. A people's worth derives in the first instance from the nature of the races that go to make up the mixture, then from the race that predominates in the mixture. Racial character is determined by the proportions in which races are represented in the overall mixture. There are, in relation to the Germans, two types of foreigner. Firstly, there are those of a related kind with the same racial mixture but in different proportions. This kind of foreigner can ally with Germans and marry with them. Other foreigners, on the other hand, namely negroes and Jews are racially totally incompatible with people of German blood. Therefore, the law made a distinction between nationality and freedom of the city. No racial conditions were imposed in order that a man be recognised as of German nationality. The law granted nationality. But in order to obtain freedom of the city, it was necessary to be of German or related blood and to show by one's conduct the intentions and qualities needed by a faithful servant of the German peoples and the Reich. Only those entitled to freedom of the city had any political rights. The law protected German blood. Marriage and extra-marital sexual relations were forbidden between Jews and those having freedom of the city. Thus, laws created a caste structure.

The German people formed a community because it was not composed of individuals grouped together by law or by the state while remaining individuals with their own private thoughts, but of people whose innermost selves were really co-ordinated one with the other. Everyone, in effect, was imbued with the common, objective spirit of the German people, the *Volksgeist*, which in each person came from his blood, and therefore they formed a genuine spiritual community or perhaps more accurately a communion, a living reality, harmoniously attuned to each other in a single community of German people. The *Volk* is, as it were, a person with a body, a will, an instinctive wisdom that imbues each individual, and an infallibility, because everything that it becomes conscious of, expresses its desire and need for life and strength. And God, in moving towards perfection, is immanent in the *Volk*. Man is, therefore, not an individual but a single cell among many that go to make up the community. He has no rights beyond the interests of the community. 'Legality means being useful to the people.' This is what German law (30 January 1936) says officially: 'Whatever is useful to the community of the German people is just. Whatever is detrimental to the people is unjust.' National (i.e. racial) interests prevail over any others. Morality is based on usefulness to the community. Anything is permissible which will ensure that the German *Volk* rules the world. Morality and law are both dictated by the spirit of the people. It is this *Volksgeist* which establishes the value judgements from which the *Führung* is derived.

The *Führung* is the control and leadership of the people. The Führer strides out ahead of the people showing them the way. The whole race follows him (*Gefolgschaft*),[16] as his faithful and devoted followers, his *Antrustions*.[16] Both Führer and people are closely united by the *Volksgeist* which resides in each of them, but especially within the Führer. And so there is a mystical union of Führer and people. 'I am wholly within you as you are wholly in me.' Thus the German can follow blindly the way indicated by his Führer but he remains the freest of men since he is only following himself, because he himself also embodies the *Volksgeist*. The Führer is the man most imbued with the *Volksgeist*. He is the conscience, will and mouthpiece of the people. He is like the *Volk*, infallible. Every second that passes, the *Volk* is creating the state and the Führer is expressing the will of the *Volk*. His power does not come from the people who have less *Volksgeist* than him. His power is a personal, charismatic one that represents the reign of his personal will, above laws and contrary to them. The people are aware of and recognise his power and do not confer it on him. However, this power is that of a guide. The Führer shows the way, he does not give orders. The Germans are not his subjects but his followers.

Being supremely imbued with the *Volksgeist*, the Führer has all the *Führung*. Thus, laws passed on 24 March 1933 and 30 January 1934 acknowledged his power of modifying the Constitution by the ordinary legislative channels. The Führer held legislative power. The Reichstag, in 1935, no longer had the initiative when it came to passing laws and could only deliberate on subjects submitted to it by its president who was appointed by the Führer. The distinction between head of state and head of government was abolished by a law passed on 1 August 1934 after Hindenburg's death. The Führer had recourse to a plebiscite by way of a referendum, but he alone had the initiative and the people did not approve the laws passed or measures taken by the Führer but simply said that they were following the Führer and were well and truly his *Gefolgschaft*.

The Führer freely appointed and dismissed advisers who only intervened at his bidding. The main advisers were his ministers. He appointed and dismissed agents to carry out under his control acts of *Führung*. The Führer's decisions did not tolerate any opposition from individuals even though they might have recourse to legal proceedings. If the Führer should falter or show signs of weakness, another man with more *Volksgeist* within him can rise up against him and take his place. However, the power of the Führer while in office was totalitarian. Because of the *Volksgeist*, he monopolised political power. On 14 July 1933, a law banned all political parties except the Führer's. On 30 January 1934, a law stripped the German regions of their rights to sovereignty and of their autonomy and reduced them to the level of mere administrative districts. The Führer concentrated in himself all legislative, executive and judicial powers and especially the power of repression which he exercised without the intervention of courts of law. The Führer was constantly evolving and formulating rules of law implicit in the *Volksgeist*.

The key instrument of the *Führung* is the German Workers' National Socialist Party, the N.S.D.A.P. or Nazi Party, the only party allowed after 14 July 1933. Under the law passed on 1 December 1933, the Nazi Party 'is the trustee of the German idea of the state and is indissolubly linked with the state'. In fact, Adolf Hitler, the Party Führer, was Führer and Chancellor of the Reich; Rudolph Hess, the Führer's Party representative and minister without portfolio of the Reich; the *Gauleiter* or party district heads were often also *Statthalter*[17] or top officials in the Reich. However, local Party agents were not generally district *Landräte*[18] or *Bürgmeisters* of the communes. Party and state have a common spirit and a common objective. They are united but they are not absorbed by each other. The Party is a corporate body by public law according to the law of 1 December 1933. It is an autonomous body subject exclusively to the control of the Führer. It has legislative power appropriate for formulating its own laws. The Führer draws up the Party's rules not as Chancellor of the Reich but as Führer of the Party. The treasurer is one of the Führer's representatives. Disciplinary committees are the party's affair. It is separate from the state but this is no drawback because the Party has more *Volksgeist* than the State and collaborates with it.

The Party's exact role is to further the spread and pre-dominance of the *Volksgeist* by propagating Nazi ideas in order to facilitate the *Führung*. It is especially responsible for education, moral and spiritual instruction by creating a certain kind of man. It is a kind of 'church' whose members have the characteristics of a sacerdotal body engaged in religious propaganda.

In addition, the Party controls municipal administration according to the law enacted on 30 January 1935. A Party commissioner approves the municipal charter, and for every post of burgomaster or his deputy puts forward three candidates to the state official in charge of nominations. He appoints members of the municipal council himself.

State officials assist Party agents at their request. The law of 20 December 1934 granted the Party's Führer and his chief officials the same protection offered to the state's Führer, to his ministers and to *Statthalter*.

The Party acts through its storm troopers, the SA, and its security forces or SS, the Führer's personal guard; the 'Hitler Youth' organisations; the Women's Union; the Students' Union; the Union of German Doctors and similar unions for lawyers, teachers, civil servants, technicians; and through the Workers' Front etc.

In 1932, the Party had 1.5 million members. In 1933, 2 million more members were added. From 1 May 1933 onwards, the Party could recruit only from members of Hitler Youth. However, in November 1935, members of the nationalist organisation the 'Steel Helmet', which was disbanded, were incorporated into the Party. At that point in time, membership was 3–4 million. Every new member was sworn in because the Party is a social order.

The State was the Führer's means of achieving the ends of Nazism, but Nazism was the desire to create a new kind of man and a new society of orders which would have become a society of castes. 'Our movement is even more than a religion: it is the will to bring about a new creation of mankind' (Hitler). In its first phase, a superior order in the new society was to be selected by the degree to which a follower rallied round the Führer, giving evidence of how much *Volksgeist* was in him and therefore how racially suitable he was. 'This is the infallible method of finding the men one needs because every man only receives what he has been granted deep within him' (from a speech at Nuremberg, 3 September 1933). Warmhearted acceptance of the Nazi ideal is a surer sign than outward appearances and distinctive physical characteristics. From such men, Hitler built a new order-based society. Put in the highest, privileged positions, these men would allow him by their blind obedience to fashion the new men.

'These men, to whom the N.S.D.A.P. granted rank and power, to whom it gave everything a real man could want from life, must on the other hand recognise and keep close to their hearts the feeling that they are a part of the Party-order for better or worse and that they owe it their unconditional obedience.'[19]

These men, themselves improved by a life of physical exercise, are destined to found a new generation which, having been brought up from very early childhood as leaders, will become a new race of overlords, made to command. The order-based society will thus be transformed into one made up of castes. Men, in fact, are divided into gods and beasts. What Nazism wanted to do was create a race of gods, to renew human nature in order to achieve 'the real golden age'.

'The selection of the new controlling class is my struggle for power. Whoever rallies round me becomes one of my chosen followers by this profession of faith and the way in which it is proclaimed. The immense significance of our long, hard struggle for power is that it allows a new generation of overlords to blossom forth, men called to steer not only the destiny of the German people but also that of the whole world.'

This new man will be characterised by the will to dominate, to direct and in all circumstances behave like a master. He will develop this tendency systematically to the point where it becomes a passion. For example, he will learn to ride a horse in order to enjoy exercising absolute domination over a living creature. He will be belligerent, fervent and cruel. He will allow himself to be carried along by natural instincts, all of which are good because they stem from his blood and in succumbing to them the overlord becomes the intrument of the obscure will of his race. However, for all this, he needs to avoid all thoughts and culture that might weaken him. 'Knowledge just corrupts the young.' The selected child will therefore receive instruction in special schools—Junkers schools initially, then *Ordensburgen* schools later. In these, his character, heart and body will harden. He will become a 'God-Man', instrumental in fulfilling the purpose of his race with which he retains a mystical bond. With his peers he will form the 'pure-blooded order' (Himmler).

Even before this generation was fashioned, Hitler was outlining a caste-structured society. The SS formed in 1929 as Hitler's bodyguard and numbering by 1931 some 10,000 men responsible for special missions, were regarded by the Germans as an order in themselves within the Party and at the top of it, but they were an order based on racial characteristics and purity of blood as a guarantee of purity of feelings and ideas. Members of the SS had to be at least six feet tall, be of absolutely pure German blood, be thorough-going Nazis, and their genealogy had to be traceable back to 1750.

By the second generation, the society created is not dissimilar to the Greek cities where hereditary aristocracies were served by a strong underpinning of helots. Between five and ten per cent of the population were to be given hereditary rank and position well above all the others and were to govern them while the other ninety to ninety-five per cent had to revere, obey and work for them. Hitler brought a degree of diversity and sharper definition to this general structure. He would talk of 'classes' but in describing them it was clear that he meant 'orders'. The new Nazi society was to comprise four orders: a high National Socialist nobility, 'the pure-blooded order', 'selected by combat'; then the hierarchy of a second order which would have replaced the Party, all of whom would be true Germans, of pure German stock; then 'the great mass of anonymous people . . . those who collectively carry out orders, destined to remain minor orders forever'; and lastly come 'individuals of foreign stock reduced to a state of subjection whom we might quite simply call . . . slaves'. We can see that, because race, heredity and purity of blood as a source of spiritual purity are the basis of this classification, we are dealing here, in fact, with castes as regards the first two orders and groups of castes for the last two.

The Roehm affair has been used to cast doubt on the sincerity of Hitler's followers in organising an order-based, then caste-based, society. Roehm, the head of the SA, was dissatisfied, as were many SA members, with arrangements Hitler made with the big capitalists who had financed his rise to power. The Führer, in effect, refused to nationalise the big industrial and commercial firms, even forbade joint management, allowed private ownership of the means of production to continue and extolled the virtues of the private initiative of the businessman. Roehm tried a *coup d'état*, was arrested on 30 June 1934 and executed in his cell. The SA were purged and reduced to a third of their numbers.

The whole Party was purged. It has been deduced from this that the Führer wished to preserve the class system and the preponderance of big bourgeois capitalists. However, one must remember that Hitler in power was still struggling fiercely against the Jews, the Communists, the Social-Democrats and the Catholics and could not add to the

11

number of his opponents. Above all, Hitler was seriously threatened by the enemy within, not only by Roehm's personal animosity, not only by opposition to his political tactics, but by the fact that, within the Party, the fluid type of order structure was beginning to give way to the more rigid type. From 1933 onwards, about a million Nazi militants had been well provided for, enjoying the luxury of elegant villas and expensive motor cars, and organising or attending lavish receptions. They lost their revolutionary zeal and original strength of faith. The Roehm affair was the occasion for both a purge and a re-awakening of political fervour. It has various aspects to it but it does seem to mark a stage in the creation of a society of orders.

4. *Union of Soviet Socialist Republics*

The Bolsheviks' aim was certainly not to organise an order-based society. They wanted to put an end to the domination of the capitalist, bourgeois class by dictatorship of the proletariat and, with the latter imposing the socialisation of the means of production, to bring about a classless society which would, once and for all, bring to an end man's exploitation of his fellow man. According to Lenin, commenting on Marx and Engels, the state is the product of society at a certain stage in its development. When antagonism between social classes gets to the stage where they are irreconcilable, the state comes into being to prevent the classes from fighting with each other. However, the state is, perforce, the organ by which one class dominates the others who can only free themselves by violent revolution. By its very nature, the state consists of a group of specialist civil servants and officials, a group of people apart from the rest of the population and above them, and having the regular army, the police and taxation at their disposal. It is a bureaucracy.

The proletariat must therefore first of all seize power by violence. Then it must shatter the bureaucratic and military machinery, suppress the regular army and replace it by the people under arms, abolish the bureaucracy and put in its place temporary officials, chosen from among all the citizens, elected and able to be dismissed by the people, remunerated by a 'normal worker's wage' with simplified duties open to everyone in turn, which are no longer the 'special duties of a special category of people'. The people have to organise themselves into workers' and soldiers' communes whose powers will be concentrated and exercised by soviets of elected representatives. These soviets send delegates to the capital, to a national soviet which co-ordinates the activities of all the individual soviets, leads the struggle against the capitalists, nationalises the railways and factories etc. The state becomes the 'proletariat organised into the dominant class', 'the revolutionary dictatorship of the proletariat'. The dictating proletariat will organise socialism. The means of production will belong to the whole of society. Goods produced will be shared out according to how much social effort is contributed by the individual, according to the principle of 'Equal pay for equal work'. However, gradually, the division of labour will disappear and with it the antagonism that exists between intellectual and manual work. Thereupon, work will become the prime need of human existence. Each man will work willingly according to his abilities and there will be as a result an immense expansion in productivity. Each man will be able to be paid not only according to the work he has done but also according to his needs. Socialism will be left behind and communism become established. When this happens, with classes also having disappeared because there will no longer be any distinction made between men according to their role in the production process, men will grow accustomed to observing, without being forced to, the elementary rules of social life, and, together with social classes, the machinery for social constraint, the state itself, will disappear. The aim of the Russian Revolution was to achieve a communist society, without classes and without the machinery of the state.

In the seizure of power by the proletariat and in the transition from capitalism to socialism, then to communism, the communist Bolshevik Party was to play a leading role. The Bolshevik Party was the vanguard of the working class, its conscious, marxist, arm, equipped with a knowledge of the laws of social development and class warfare, and therefore able to guide the working class and direct its political struggles. However, within the Party, a small permanent body of professional revolutionaries was given the special duty of organising and maintaining continuity of labour. This group was to organise the Party and the proletariat according to the principle of democratic centralisation, with a single body of laws, a single controlling organism, a single code of discipline obligatory for each and every Party member, which allowed millions of workers to be formed into the army that was the working class, hierarchically-structured, disciplined and ready for the fight ahead and for victory.

The Revolution in October 1917 effectively crushed large-scale private ownership of the means of production. It established a proletarian dictatorship and attempted to build a proletarian society on the basis of complete equality at a very low standard of living. Stringent rationing was imposed in an attempt to equalise consumption. The living area of houses and apartments was measured and the available space shared out equally. All social ranks were abolished, all wages were reduced to the average level of a working man's pay. In April 1922, workers earned on average 5.71 roubles a month, civil servants 5.74 roubles a month.

However, at the same time, the Bolsheviks were, without

knowing it, laying the foundations for a society made up of orders. There was a proletariat dictatorship over the other classes of society that were still in existence, but at the same time, a dictatorship by the Party over the proletariat, and within the Party itself, dictatorship by the old professionals, the 'old guard', like Lenin, Zinoviev, Kamenev, Rykov, Tomsky, Trotsky, Stalin and so on, over the rest of the Party. On principle a Party congress was held every year while Lenin was alive. It elected a central committee that met three or four times a year and delegated power to it. In fact, power was exercised by the Politburo and by the secretary of the central committee. Theoretically, power within the nation belonged to all the people and they exercised it through their soviets. In practice though, all organisations were subordinate to the Party, and the most important governmental decisions had to be signed jointly by the head of the government and the first Secretary of the Party. Only the Party determined the proletariat's interests.

In October 1917, the Bolsheviks must have numbered about 240,000 or 0.2 per cent of the total population; when Lenin died in 1924, the total was about one million. The fact that they had real power gave this minority a position of some eminence in the new Russian society. There were two ranks; a lower one for ordinary Party members and a higher rank for the 'old guard' and their immediate auxiliaries. Lenin, on 16 March 1922, declared that the 'old guard' determined the proletarian policy of the Party. As it was power, engendered by the strength of one's belief in marxism-leninism, that would determine one's social rank and not, as before, private ownership of the means of production, the basic principle of an order-based society had already been introduced into the Russia of the soviets and the first phase of such a society, based on strength of faith in an ideology, was being outlined.

The march towards the formation of a society of orders of

the rigid type now proceeded without interruption. After the civil war (1919–20), the Bolshevik Party began to change in character. On the one hand, the strength of faith of a good number of its members was decreasing. Secure in their jobs, they became bureaucratic in spirit, lost touch with the masses and strove to derive material advantages from their positions. On the other hand, there were factors militating against the attempted egalitarian, proletarian movement. It became necessary to stimulate zeal by differences in income and rations. It was necessary to keep competent people in office and to bring in others. It was, in short, necessary to restore and develop a social hierarchy. At the same time as the desperate situation forced Lenin to adopt the 'new economic policy' (NEP) in the summer of 1921, ambitious careerists and opportunists tried to make their way into the Party solely for the social advantages that it offered and not because of their belief in marxism-leninism and the Revolution. The 'old guard' was forced to let them in. Lenin was uneasy about this. At the end of 1921 he launched a great 'Party Week'. One hundred and sixty-six thousand members were excluded from this and the Party strength was cut by 23 per cent. However, from March 1922 onwards, after Lenin's first heart attack, there was a rush of petits-bourgeois.

The major changes that took place in the Party resulted from divisions within the 'old guard'. After Lenin's death, its members squabbled over power. Stalin succeeded in seizing it in 1925, then in getting rid of Trotsky in 1927. But he only succeeded by using the Party and State bureaucrats in his fight against the policies of the 'apparatus', against the Bolsheviks. After Lenin's death, Stalin had 200,000 to 250,000 new Party members enrolled in order to swamp the old Bolsheviks. In this way he was able to get rid of members of the 'old guard' one by one. The 17th Party Congress in January 1934 can be called the 'Victors'

Congress'. From 1934 to 1938 the Stalinist bureaucracy exterminated almost every one of the revolutionaries from 1917. Only Stalin himself was left. In January 1934, the 17th Congress still comprised about 23 per cent of old Bolsheviks who had joined the Party before the Revolution. In March 1939, the 18th Congress had only 2.4 per cent. At the 17th Congress 26 per cent of the delegates had joined the Party since the civil war; at the 18th Congress, the figure was 80 per cent and 268 of the 333 top Party officials (80 per cent) had joined the Party since Lenin's death. The 18th Congress decided to introduce into the Party the highest possible number of members of the intelligentsia, engineers and officials, in order to involve them more closely in the regime's responsibilities. The new members were increasingly civil servants, far removed from manual work and quite often scornful of workers and peasants. Little by little they took control of all representative and administrative posts. At the 15th Party Congress (December 1927) 18.4 per cent of the delegates were still workers coming from their factories. At the 17th Congress (January 1934) the proportion had dropped to 9.3 per cent. There is no information given for the 18th Congress (March 1939). However, it is known that at that time, there was not a single worker among the 139 members of the central committee. The Party had become the expression and the instrument of the dominant bureaucracy. On 1 January 1945 the Party had 5,700,000 members, on 1 October 1952 6,882,445 and in 1964 perhaps some 9,000,000. This was approximately three to four per cent of the country's total population. Of these, about 750,000 to 1,000,000 made up the political bureaucracy, 'elite of Party workers were included in this category', i.e. those who exercised power. The others were the executive, administrative and technical element. The former were the governing group, the members of the 'apparatus', the *apparatchiks* recruited mostly from the communist youth or *Komsomol*, thoroughly indoctrinated, having hardly had time to learn anything else, and having always benefited, in the course of their studies, from bonus marks or gift diplomas, by virtue of their marxist-leninist sentiments and their activity within the Party. They were a social group of privileged persons constituting the superior order of the society, a 'supernobility'.

Below them the other Party members formed the 'organisation'. They were at every level within the Party, subordinate to those members of the apparatus in charge at that level. Socially they constituted collectively an order that was inferior to the 'apparatus'. Members of the 'organisation' were scientists, administrators, engineers, soldiers of high rank, some of whom had left the ranks of the *apparatchiks* and others were simply technicians.

Up to 1934 and the total triumph of Stalinist bureaucracy, the technicians consisted mostly of the former Russian elites, under the watchful eye of the police and held in check by the 'apparatus'. After 1934 a series of purges eliminated a large number of them. They were replaced by a new, hastily trained generation of specialists produced by workers' colleges, the pupils of 'red professors' who themselves had been rapidly taught. These technicians were, in general, members of the Party but not members of the 'apparatus'.

The war increased the role and importance of the technicians. The death of Stalin brought relative and progressive liberalisation. Towards the sixties they were able to challenge the *apparatchiks*. Those who rose against the dictatorship of the 'apparatus' were the economists, advisers on the Plan, administrators in industry, commerce, transport and building, imbued with the principle of profitability, struck by 'the absurdity of a system in which a parasitic caste of a million privileged individuals prevents the country's economy from functioning rationally', and impressed by the efficiency of the methods in use in the semi-liberal economies of neo-capitalist countries. Then it was the turn of the following groups to rise against the dictatorship, the agronomists, senior officials of the ministers of Agriculture responsible for the *sovkhozes*[20] and the *kolkhozes*;[21] the head functionaries of state; the diplomats; the scientists, research workers, civil and military engineers; the members of the institutions of higher education; the jurists, professors, magistrates, barristers; the intelligentsia of philosophers, writers and artists.

In theory, at every level within the Party the 'apparatus' was elected by the 'organisation'. In practise, however, the 'apparatus' recruited its own members. It consisted of the Praesidium of the Central Committee of the Communist Party, with seventeen members; the central Secretariat composed of a first Secretary and nine Secretaries for ideology, administration, agitation, the supervision of ministries etc.; the Central Committee of the Party with a membership of 175 and a further 155 candidate members, nominated by the Praesidium at the suggestion of the 'trained personnel' of the secretariat; half of these were *apparatchiks*, the other half top civil servants, academics, engineers and high-ranking soldiers except for four workers who were *stakhanovistes* or members of the working-class aristocracy. The provinces of large towns, districts, localities, large governing bodies, industrial enterprises, the *sovkhozes* and the *kolkhozes* and the capitals of the Republic each had their Party organisation, with a Party headquarters and a secretariat.

The Party hierarchy was the only true hierarchy of power. The state apparatus was simply the executive machinery for the party apparatus. According to Article 126 of the 1936 Constitution, the Party was the 'governing nucleus of every workers' organisation both social and state-oriented'.

On principle, according to the 1936 constitution the Union of Soviet Socialist Republics, the USSR, was a socialist state composed of workers and peasants, and all power in the state belonged to the workers in town and country represented by the soviets made up of workers as deputies. A pyramid structure of elected soviets, from village, district and town, each having full powers at its respective level, culminated in the supreme soviet of the USSR itself. 'The highest organ of the state's power.' This consisted of two groups, the Soviet of the Union with one deputy for every 300,000 inhabitants and the Soviet of nationalities. Altogether the two had a membership of about 3,000 people. Workers and peasants had, bit by bit, been more or less excluded from them. In 1950, they accounted for only 6.9 per cent. The Supreme Soviet consisted of a huge body of Party and state bureaucrats. It met for only two short sessions a year and delegated its powers to a Praesidium.

The Praesidium was a collective head of state made up of a president, fifteen vice-presidents (one for each federated Republic), a secretary and fifteen ordinary members. It nominated ministers and the people's commissars, it legislated, decided on peace or war and on matters of diplomatic relations. This extremely powerful body was largely composed of *apparatchiks* and was like a branch of the secretariat of the central Committee.

The government consisted of a Praesidium of the Council of Ministers (a President of the Council, a senior vice-president and eight other vice-presidents), sixteen ministers, twenty-four state committees. Half the members were *apparatchiks*, the others technicians. The government governed as the Party directed. Ministerial decrees had the force of law but all decisions had to be signed jointly by the first secretary to the Party and by the President of the Council. Party directives and Party control, or in other words, power wielded by *apparatchiks*, was prevalent everywhere. And the same was true at every level of administration and in all those mass organisations that Lenin called 'driving belts'; communist youth movements or *Komsomol*; trades unions in which most of the important positions were held by *apparat-chiks*; writers', journalists' and artists' unions etc.; the central committee of the sporting bodies and organisations etc, right across the board, the *apparatchiks* were at the heart of the power structure.

This political bureaucracy had become an unbridled strength dominating the mass of people. It was a powerful group of specialists who organised production and distribution in such a way as to favour the privileged groups that were most indispensable in defence, industry, technical matters and science. For example, the bureaucracy commanded all means of production, imposed hard labour, forbade strikes and demonstrations, drew off a substantial part of the surplus value created by labour in order to convert it into means of production but also for its own personal use. The workers had, little by little, been deprived of any participation in the management of concerns. A decree on 29 November 1917 gave the workers the right to control production, sales, purchasing, and the financial side of an undertaking. Factory committees were to elect a council in every town and a Pan-Russian Council in Petrograd, in order to control the economy. But meetings of these committees became rarer and rarer. Control passed into the hands of *troikas* made up of the head of the firm, the Party secretary and the trade union secretary within the firm. From 1927 and the first five-year Plan onwards, the bureaucracy strengthened the powers of managers. In 1937 the *troikas* were suppressed and the running of concerns was put solely into the hands of the head of the firm who had total responsibility and power of decision, subject to the control and the directives issued by the Party.

According to the *Principles of Soviet Constitutional Law*, published in Moscow in 1947 by the Minister of Justice: 'The most important principle of the socialist organisation of labour is that this labour should be controlled by one man only.' 'Control by an individual as applied in the industrial context means that special managers are put at the head of every industrial enterprise and every economic body appointed by the competent state organism. They are the absolute controllers of the enterprise, and enjoy the complete confidence of the governmental authorities'. The technician is master, therefore, under the control of the *apparatchik*.

These changes were sanctioned by modifications to political formulae. The 1936 Constitution granted total power to the Soviets of workers' representatives. The 20th Party Congress, in October 1961, declared that, henceforth, society had no classes at all, and therefore that the time had come to change from the 'proletariat dictatorship' to 'collective, communist, auto-adminstration', to a 'communal state' to 'the state of the entire people'. The Communist Party, in the 1952 statutes, instead of being defined as it was previously as 'the organised vanguard of this country's working class' was said to be a 'free, militant association of communists with a common spirit, that brings together people from the working class, the manual peasantry and intellectual workers.'

As a result of this new distribution of power, this differentiation of functions that derived from a new division of labour, a social stratification emerged that was different from every expectation. Many writers have noted the fact; Milovan Djilas, in 1957, talks of a 'new class', the political bureaucracy 'made into an organisation of a special kind, characterised by a special discipline based on the identical philosophical and ideological viewpoints of its members'. It was a class unified by its 'beliefs and iron discipline'. Nicolas Rutych, in 1961, believed it was a mistake 'to try to find a new class within a social structure that did not admit class', but he also points out the existence of a bureaucratic political minority, the Party secretaries, at the head of the machinery of the soviets and the army, the instrument of the

State's security. This minority sets itself up as a superior stratum of society which 'soon stands apart from the people and, moreover, begins to consider itself as a completely different entity to the people'. Some time before Rutych, Kakovsky had denounced 'the governing côterie' which 'has managed to become an immovable and inviolable oligarchy. It has taken the place of class and the Party'. Leon Trotsky too, as early as 1936, put it more clearly in his *Revolution Betrayed*:

> 'In the proletarian state where the capitalistic accumulation of wealth is forbidden for members of the governing Party, differentiation is firstly by function, then it becomes a social thing. I am not saying that it becomes class differentiation, I am saying that it becomes social differentiation. . . . The social category which, without providing direct productive labour, commands, administers, governs, metes out punishment and reward . . . must be estimated at some five or six million souls.'[22]

Many observers, therefore, were agreed in pointing out that new social strata had come into being which were something different from social classes. However, because there were no comparable situations against which to judge this, they failed to recognise those strata for what they were, namely social orders and 'estates'. The Communist Party in the USSR had certainly become as early as the thirties and the emergence of Stalin, and probably even earlier, a social order consisting of at least two 'estates' hierarchically arranged with the political bureaucracy of *apparatchiks* on top and the technicians just below them.

Many of the characteristic features of a social order may be found in these social groups. Firstly, there is the tendency towards co-optation, heredity and endogamy. Even Trotsky remarked on it: 'As for the young bureaucrats they are schooled and selected by the older generation of bureaucrats, often from among their own offspring.' 'Husband and wife, sometimes also son and daughter, frequently belong to the bureaucratic apparatus.'[23] 'A visitor to Russia in 1959 and 1961 was struck by the number of young people occupying within the administration, or even within scientific bodies responsible to the Academy of Sciences, positions that were far and away above their abilities. They enjoyed a standard of living that was quite incompatible with their salaries and their success, as well as their life style, could only, in the final analysis, be explained by the fact that they were the sons of senior bureaucrats, all of whom were members of the Party. In the army, general officers were all Party members often in high positions, and had all been trained and brought up by the Party. As a group it tended towards endogamy. In 1955 Marshall Jukov, a member of the Communist Party Praesidium and Minister of National Defence, had one of his daughters married to the son of Marshal Vassilevski, another to the grandson of Marshal Voroshilov. Offices tended towards a hereditary system. In the early 1940s officers' schools were set up under the invocation of Suvarov.[24] The *Suvarovzy*, trained from the age of eight, were almost exclusively all sons of officers. Officers enjoyed privileges, had 'courts of honour'[25] and, for marshals and generals, there were country estates and houses. Officers were given social symbols, a special sabre and, for generals, six different uniforms resplendent with braid, velvet and gold brocades. Furthermore, since 3 January 1939, the form of words for the military oath had been modified. The words 'revolution' and 'revolutionary' had been cut out as well as the obligation to 'devote all one's thoughts and deeds to the great cause of liberating the workers'. The soldier was no longer fighting 'in the service of socialism and the brotherhood of peoples' but in order to 'overthrow his enemies'. No longer did the soldier pledge his word 'before the working classes of Russia and the whole world'. On 25 February 1947 the Constitution was amended. The expression 'red army of workers and peasants' was replaced by the 'armed forces of the USSR'.

Within the growing number of bureaucratic organisms, there was a sharp increase in the number of social symbols or outward signs of one's place in the functional hierarchy, which, in this kind of society, corresponds to a social hierarchy. From the early 1940s onwards grades were allocated as were distinctive badges and uniforms for civil service personnel. On 28 May 1943 it was the turn of Foreign Affairs personnel whose grades were indicated by shoulder straps woven in silver thread and bearing golden emblems, and diplomatic rank by gold stars. In succession followed, in 1943, railway personnel and magistrates in the department of public prosecutions; in 1945 the police, the Registrar General's office and the public Records Office; in 1947 management and technical staff employed in inland navigation, the coal mining industry, geological services, iron smelting. Then, in the years following, came metal workers, the merchant navy, financial bodies and banks, the Post and Telecommunications officers, the state Assay Office, water works etc. The outward signs of a structured, hierarchical society, one based on a system of orders, were multiplying.

The USSR showed, therefore, many symptoms of a society of orders in the process of being formed, based on the principle of adherence to a schema inspired by marxism-leninism, and engendering passive obedience to a totalitarian bureaucracy whose members were co-opted, hierarchically arranged and tending towards heredity and endogamy. It was a bureaucracy that had seized power and, by means of this power which was based on a doctrine passing for a science, had won special social esteem, honour and an elevated rank in society.

Notes to Chapter Ten

1. *L'Ami du Peuple*, a daily.
2. Periodical of the revolutionary J. R. Hebert.
3. Periodical of Elysée Loustallot.
4. There were ten battalions to each of the six legions of the Paris National Guard during the revolution.
5. Collot d'Herbois, 'Sur les mitraillades de Lyon', *Moniteur*, XIV, p. 189.
6. At the battle of Wissembourg in 1793 the French beat the Austrians and Prussians.
7. Châlier in the Club Central of Lyons, 21 March 1793, 23 March 1793, quoted by H. Taine in *Les Origines de la France contemporaine*, Paris, 1899, Vol. I pp. 81, 83.
8. *Mercure de France*, 7 April 1792.
9. Mussolini, *Doctrine of Fascism*, Ardita, Rome, 1935 p. 9.
10. Mussolini, *idid.*, p. 40.
11. 'musketeers'.
12. 'machine-gunners'.
13. Mussolini, *Doctrine of Fascism*, pp. 10–11.
14. Mussolini, speech to the General Staff Conference of Fascism, *ibid.*, p. 38.
15. Mussolini, *ibid.*, p. 27.
16. Significantly, *Gefolgschaft* and *Antrustiones* are both terms belonging to the period of the barbarian invasions, and disappeared ca. 750, with the development of feudal lordship. *Gefolgschaft* was the attachment of warriors to the king, among whom the upper class of *Antrustiones* were in the king's immediate vicinity. *Antrustio*: he who swears trust or fidelity. Cf. Du Fresne: *Glossarium mediae et infimae latinitatis* and Bruno Gebhart, *Handbuck der deutschen Geschichte*, 9th ed., Stuttgart, 1970, Vol. I, pp. 709, 723, 737f., 743.
17. Equivalent of the French 'prefect'.
18. Correspond to Eng. 'sheriff' or French 'sub-prefect'.
19. Robert Ley, *Der Weg zur Ordenburg*, Munich 1943.
20. 'government farm'.
21. 'collective farm'.
22. Leon Trotsky, *The Revolution Betrayed*, Faber and Faber, London, 1937, p. 101.
23. *Ibid.*, p. 134–35.
24. Russian Field-Marshal, 1729–1800, reformer of the Russian army.
25. Borrowed from the Russian Imperial Army. Tried officers for offences that demean the prestige of the officer corps.

Chapter Eleven

The Technocratic Order in the twentieth century

Technocratic societies of orders are those in which technicians hold an essential part of political and administrative power and form, through the exercise of this power, social groups that are ranked in the highest echelons of the social hierarchy. It is in relation to these groups that the whole scale of social strata and social groups is organised, and they provide society with the basic principles of its ideology together with its moral and social values. When technical men become conscious of the extreme importance of their functions within society and strive to use these functions in order to exercise political and administrative power, they become 'technocrats'. Technocratic societies differ from 'philosophic' societies of orders in that they spring from a concrete situation, namely the pre-eminence of technology at a particular moment in time, instead of being an attempt to realise an overall view of the universe, man and society. Every 'philosophic' order in the nineteenth and twentieth centuries has, however, certain technocratic aspects and so these two types of society, actually quite distinct, have often been confused.

The idea of a society dominated by technical men and scientists, in so far as science and technology are a function of each other, came about with the advent of the Industrial Revolution, with coal and iron replacing wood and water, with the application of the power of steam to machinery, and the proliferation of the latter, as soon as small sections of humanity began to enter the industrial era at the end of the eighteenth century and the beginning of the nineteenth century in England, France and Germany. Students of technocracy like to call to mind Count Saint-Simon (1760–1825) who, in the first quarter of the nineteenth century had a clear conception of a technocratic society, and they recall his formula: 'Substitute the administration of things for the government of men.' The technocratic idea can also be found in the work of his disciple Auguste Comte (1798–1857) from 1830 onwards. Augustin Cournot (1801–77) developed his theories, particularly in 1872, on the inevitable mechanisation of mankind, the progressive substitution in society of the rational for the vital, and the conditioning of mankind by the technical milieu.

However, in fact, the technocratic movement did not spring from theoretical considerations and it seems that neither Saint-Simon, Comte nor Cournot were read very much by the technocrats themselves. Technocracy did not even come directly perhaps from the industrial era and the transformations of capitalism, although industrialisation and and neo-capitalism were essential conditions for it. It appears that it is with war that technocracy originates. First of all, there was the First World War, 1914–18. The vital necessity of manufacturing massive quantities of increasingly efficient war materials gave engineers of every order a more important role in society than they had ever had before. The need to feed, clothe, and transport millions of fighting men, often also to ensure that supplies were brought to whole populations, as well as the necessity of keeping up the morale of the soldier in the rear by propaganda: all of this gave powers of decision and influence over government policies and representative assemblies, to the administrators, and directors of administrative offices; in the first place to general staff soldiers and senior administrative officers of the Quartermaster General's staff, but also later civil administrators, such as they had never had until then. The state was forced to intervene, moreover, in every area of economic, social, intellectual and scientific activity and, in order to do this, it had to delegate special powers to technical experts in administration. The economic and social upheavals aggravated by war, together with economic crises such as the great world slump in 1929, accentuated this process. The Second World War, 1939–45, and its consequences accelerated and augmented it. It is great wars that have, in countries of Western European civilisation, whether in Europe itself or overseas, created the age of administrators.

To my knowledge, in the twentieth century, no society has yet been wholly a technocratic one. The one that comes nearest is the USSR except that marxist-leninist ideology and the attempt to go from a proletarian dictatorship to a classless society force us to classify it as a society of 'philosophic' orders. However, in several industrial societies or those in the process of becoming rapidly industrialised, there is a clearly defined tendency towards a technocratic system, in, for example, the United States, Great Britain, France, Italy, Germany and elsewhere.

The tendency towards a technocratic system is seen in both the private and public sectors. In the private sector, the extension and concentration of concerns has brought about a progressive fall in the proportion of factories managed directly by their owners, operating on their own capital or that provided by members of their families and a few friends, and if needs be, capital from a relatively limited number of other shareholders. Instead of one man directing the firm himself or, at least, controlling the production process, there is a growing number of businesses that have become huge combines of factories each one working for the other. Business has become integrated into horizontally-structured concentrations, grouping enterprises of the same type, e.g. steelworks of one or several regions, financially and commercially and in manufacturing methods; or in a vertical structure so that the produce of one group becomes the raw material of another, for example in coal mining, iron mines, blast furnaces, steelworks, locomotive works or shipyards etc. The nominal owners of these businesses, the shareholders, consisting, alongside large stock owners, of thousands of small shareholders have had to delegate responsibility for management and control of the technical production processes to various kinds of technicians, such as engineers in charge of manufacturing, administrative directors to organise the release of liquid capital, the recruitment and deployment of personnel throughout the firm's various levels, the concentration of raw materials at different stages in production, the movement and allocation of manufactured products, publicity, distribution and marketing. Directors, from being technical men in charge of manufacturing, have more and more become organisational specialists. Early on they were mostly engineers but increasingly they have included men with a purely legal background and, nowadays, their is a growth in the number of men with a predominantly humanities-based education because organisational problems are often mainly problems of human relationships in which the greatest difficulties lie in administering the actions of men rather than things. To these directors the owners, or shareholders, have had to delegate more and more power in the decision-making process. These directors, moreover, highly-paid but salaried men nonetheless, have tended either instinctively or rationally to reduce remuneration derived from capital by way of dividends more and more in order to use a larger share of profits to plough back into the business. They could be considered, since they largely control the means of production, as sorts of 'owners' of the business. They represent, alongside the sole legal ownership, (that of the shareholders) a kind of second ownership which would tend to put the first into a subordinate position and perhaps eliminate it altogether.

It was noticed for example that, from 1929 onwards, in the U.S.A. the economy was dominated by 200 industrial concentrations outside the banking sphere. Sixty-five of these, representing 80 per cent of the total capital employed, were controlled and directed not by their nominal, legal owners, the shareholders, but by directors who only had a very small shareholding but who, in practice, controlled the business, manipulating board meetings and general meetings at will and preserving their own power indefinitely. Admittedly the largest shareholders, the 'Sixty Families' as they were called, or more precisely the few hundred families, kept financial control, intervened at crucial moments, retained a kind of power of veto, and were able to continue to treat the directors as their deputies, but these capitalist owners moved further away from active, direct participation in the running of their firms.

In the public sector, administrative directors were more and more prompting the actions of men in government, who, in certain cases, became their spokesmen and executive agents, and they themselves sometimes acquired substantial power of decision and regulation that was equivalent to having executive and legislative power delegated to them. Firstly, the government was encroaching more and more into different sectors of the economy, either because a capitalist enterprise became unable to show a profit and thus continue operating, or because capitalist firms showed themselves incapable of satisfying the new needs of the nation and the state. The state thus took one section of the economy after the other out of the network of capitalist economic dealings. It ran economic enterprises without any concern for profit. In this way, governments, in different countries, took charge of the following operations one by one: the postal services, transport, water supply, highways, shipbuilding, public health, housing, education, social security, dams and weirs, agricultural plans, the census, reallocation of land, farming improvements, motor car manufacturing, insurance of various kinds etc. At the same time, the state was beginning to take control more and more of sectors of the economy that remained, theoretically speaking, the property of individuals or capitalist concerns, and doing so through commisions, boards, offices, laws and regulations affecting publicity, markets, labour, industrial relations, imports and exports, banking and so on and so forth. It may be pointed out also that, in all this state activity, one might add to the strictly economic sectors other more specifically social sectors, namely education, health, housing, town and country planning, leisure time activities of all kinds, such as libraries, sports stadia, swimming pools, theatres etc. Governments were not only becoming the biggest business in the land but were also regulating the lives of its citizens more and more. Governments, to a greater or lesser degree, reduced the rights of capitalist ownership and dealings on the market. Governments began to own or control the majority of instruments of production. However, for reasons similar to those in the private sector, and through the need to compensate for the inadequacies of capitalist enterprise and to co-ordinate administrative or production work in groups of businesses and offices or territories that were far bigger than those of most private enterprises, the management of firms and the administrative functions of the state were increasingly handed over to senior managers or administrative directors who were allowed very broad powers of decision and regulation without direct intervention from the national government. These men, moreover, often put up suggestions which became government projects, laws or decrees.

In this way, within most industrial states, including even the U.S.A., social groups of techno-bureaucrats had been formed with widespread powers in government and society in general. These groups were receptive to men of ability, theoretically whatever their social background, but in practice, because of their high level of technical qualifications resulting as often as not from long and arduous studies of a theoretical

kind followed by protracted spells of practical work as a pro-
bationer, recruitment was a more limited affair. The groups
were made up of a small number of men, all of whom knew each
other or, if they did not, mixed freely by virtue of the qualifications and abilities they had in common. Quite often they
worked successively, in both the private and the public
sectors, beginning sometimes with one sometimes with the
other, according to the country and the circumstances. In
France, for example, membership of these groups was drawn
from among former students of the *École Polytechnique*, the
École Centrale, the *École Nationale d'Administration*, from
Treasury officials and diplomats, and to a lesser degree, from
among former students of the *École Normale Supérieure*[1]
situated in the rue d'Ulm in Paris. All these men, gifted
with relatively high intellectual abilities and other qualities—
exceptionally so in their own eyes—assumed an attitude of
lofty, disdainful benevolence towards anyone who did not
belong to their social circles, especially the masses. Thus,
they were conscious of belonging to a social order.

They enjoyed a position of some distinction, privilege
indeed, according to some people, who used the word
'privilege' in its proper sense of advantages granted to certain
people by society, because of their particular social functions.
The techno-bureaucrats played a leading part in the
production process as well as in public administration. They
enjoyed social prestige, honour and esteem and a particularly
high rank in society. They benefited from large incomes,
without one being able to say categorically that the techno-
bureaucrats, by exploiting their scarcity value or position
drained off more than their share of society's income, to the
detriment of other social classes.

They were fully conscious of themselves and had concocted
a whole ideology, that is a collection of beliefs expressing
their ideals, their desires, hopes and fears—in which there
was nothing at all scientific despite their terminology and

jargon. The ideologies of techno-bureaucrats varied from country to country, society to society, but they had various things in common. Born of an excessive urge to dominate and their deep-seated conviction that they were the only people capable of bringing about the salvation of mankind, the technocrats professed their fundamental concern for efficiency, return on investment, and profitability. These factors implied planning, which alone would allow effort to be co-ordinated so as to get the best out of production resources, such as the world had never known, and to do away with economic crises and brakes on production. Planning would allow all mankind to enter an age of plenty. However, it also implied an increase in the state's authority in order to impose the discipline necessary for the proper functioning of economic planning. This absolute authority had to be wielded by the technocratic elite from which would emerge the great men needed to lead and guide the masses. If humanity was to enjoy happiness it would only do so if managers were in control.

The society that the technocrats were working towards was certainly a society composed of orders, because honour, esteem and the highest social rank were to be the prerogatives of the technocrats, not in the role of producers but as planners, organisers, co-ordinators, and administrators. The second highest social rank would go to their subordinates, the engineers and technicians whose function was, each man according to his station, to conduct production process as such.

Nevertheless, however much the importance and authority of the technocrats increased, one must recognise the fact that they have not yet succeeded anywhere, except in Russia, in gaining total power, in taking hold of the whole machinery of the state and in completely refashioning society. In spite of their activities, they have remained the instruments of great statesmen who made use of them; thus Franklin Roosevelt, who used the New Deal team in the U.S.A.; Léon

Blum in France in 1936, Marshal Pétain in 1941 and 1942, Mendès France in 1954, General de Gaulle in 1945 and from 1958 onwards. For these men and their political groups, the technocrats were great purveyors of ideas. Through these heads of government, the technocrats have succeeded in putting into practice a substantial number of their projects. For example, they have succeeded in going beyond the stage of 'state capitalism' in which the state only owns a minor share of the economy and in reaching the stage of 'neo-capitalism' where the state owns or controls a major part of the means of production and stipulates that workers at every level should share in the management and profits of business. However, the technocrats have not triumphed because they have been used by statesmen more than they have themselves made use of statemen.

The technocrats could not therefore be content with staying on the sidelines of out-of-date, obsolete political parties and prompting them with ideas; with figuring in ministers' offices as a source of inspiration; with lingering in the background of trades unions in the hope of influencing the masses. These institutions were set in their antiquated formulae and seemed incapable of analysing new situations. Power had to be seized.

They tried to do this although, on the whole, rather timidly. In France, for example, they tried to do so by forming 'clubs', the natural vehicle for elites to communicate with elites, particularly since certain students and former students of the *Polytechnique* or the *École Normale Supérieure* in the rue d'Ulm considered these schools themselves to be like clubs. The technocrats' clubs were small technocratic groups aimed at a limited range of heads of firms, engineers, administrators, senior civil servants, politicians and general secretaries of trades unions. They organised among themselves commissions responsible for collecting information, sifting problems, and putting forward solutions to their general assemblies. They spread their ideas through study sessions in the evenings and through books. They strove to get their members on the departmental staff of government ministries and one of them even tried to make the President of the Republic.

The two most notable clubs seem to be the '*X-Crise*' and the '*Club Jean-Moulin.*'

'*X-Crise*' was constituted in 1930 around the *Polytechnique* graduate Jean Coutrot. The Club evolved its programme from 1930 to 1934 and reached its apogee at the time of the Popular Front from 1934 to 1936. It lost influence with the defeat of the Popular Front and ceased to function altogether in 1939.

The core of its membership came from former pupils of the *École Polytechnique*, all engineers and industrialists. Engineers accounted for 42 per cent, company directors 13 per cent, industrialists 10 per cent, and senior civil servants only 4 per cent. In the beginning the Club's meetings were held in the home of Yves Bouthillier, a Treasury official who later became Minister under President Paul Reynaud, then Marshal Pétain. Coutrout became, in 1936, technical adviser to the departmental staff of Charles Spinasse, the Minister of the National Economy in the Léon Blum administration.

On the morrow of the defeat of the Popular Front, Coutrot expressed his ideas in the book *L'humanisme économique* which became the Bible of the '*X-Crise*'. From 1937 onwards, Gérard Bardet recommended employee participation, futurological research, the creation of an 'order' out of associations of state controllers checking on agreements and supervising production. The ideas of '*X-Crise*', especially on a planned economy, inspired the Léon Blum experience 1936–1937, the synarchic groups of Vichy France in 1942[2] the economic revival of Gaullist technocracy in 1945 with the Chaban-Delmas team, and the advisers of Mendès France in 1954.

On 18 May 1958, a group of former Resistance members from the 1939–45 war founded the *Club Jean-Moulin* in order to defend the Republic against General de Gaulle. In this club, it was the civil servants of 35–40 years old that predominated; 80 per cent of its members were civil servants. The others were journalists and company administrators. Among these were a number of radicals, former associates of Mendès France, former communists, members of the League of Rights of Man, leftist Catholics and socialists. Later on came teachers like Georges Vedel and Maurice Duverger. Most of the Club's members held responsible administrative positions, some having posts on the departmental staff of a government ministry. The Club never had, however, more than 550 members, but it exerted great influence through its study sessions, meetings and publications, the most important of which was *L'État et le citoyen* in 1961, put together by fifteen working parties. Although theoretically it was hostile towards the regime, in practice it could be said that: 'The Club Jean-Moulin, viewed objectively, serves to create ideas for those in power to use.' The Club tried to go further than this and create a President of the French Republic, the technocrats' own man. To this end it chose Defferre whom they supported from 1963 to 1965 but without success.

Although the technocrats have not yet been completely successful, their influence and role in society is continually on the increase. Some foresee their total success and the formation of technocratic states, governments and societies where technocrats would have complete power by virtue of their roles as organisational experts. They would, in such a situation, become the pre-eminent social order with absolute domination over the state, the power to shape society, control access to all means of production, regulate the distribution of all produce and reserve for itself a privileged share. It would be an order which, thanks to the exercise of its technical power, would hold supreme rank in a hierarchical society, which would recruit its own members and ensure that there was continuity from generation to generation. It would be a social order of such a kind that society would very soon reach the second phase of order-based societies.

It does seem in fact that industrial societies are all fixed on this course and that the technocratic society of orders could be the type of society we will have in the future.

Notes to Chapter Eleven

1. The training college of French lycée teachers and future professors, superior in standing to the Sorbonne. To have been a pupil is quoted as a title.
2. The entire French economy during the Vichy regime was organised in corporations, which, in contrast with the political organisation, were each self-governing, and constituted therefore a 'collective rule' (synarchy). Cf. Robert Aron, *The Vichy Regime*, 1940–44, Putham, London, 1958, pp. 155–6; Louis Baudin, *Esquisse de l'Economie française sous l'occupation allemande*, Paris, 1945, pp. 27–107.

Conclusion

The Big Choice

It appears that, throughout the whole world, in the long or short term according to the countries concerned, industrial civilisation is going to spread and, with it, order-based societies of a technocratic kind will have the best chances of prevailing. Already, even in 'philosophical' societies of order of the marxist-leninist kind, such as in the USSR, after the first phase in the order-based society (namely the period of fluidity in which society is organised according to intensity of faith), the second stage (in which the rigid order pattern prevails whereby society is organised according to adherence on principle to a doctrine that is the very substance of the faith), has assumed obvious technocratic characteristics despite the official marxist-leninist line. It seems that all industrial societies or all those in the process of becoming industrialised are moving towards the same type of society made up of technocratic orders, in which the state would own or control all means of production and would share out the produce. However the state would itself be in the hands of techno-bureaucrats, the directors of the organisation, who would impose a totalitarian dictatorship on the whole population in the name of planning. They would also derive social prestige, the highest honour and rank in society as well as a privileged share of the output from production from the power they would possess.

Even countries where the marxist-leninist revolution is still fresh and which are doubtless in the first phase of marxist-leninist 'philosophical' order seem already to be witnessing the emergence of the second phase in the form of a technocratic bureaucracy. This is, for example, the case in Cuba and China. Despite the enormous amount of material

189

published recently on these two countries, one cannot possibly consider oneself well informed on what is happening there. Nevertheless, it does seem that Fidel Castro's struggle against Annibal Escalante and his 'integrated revolutionary organisations' in 1962 can be explained by the fear of Fidel Castro, who was more faithful to the revolutionary ideal of the first phase in the face of a dawning technocratic bureaucratisation which escaped his control. However, Fidel Castro had, by the nature of things, become a statesman, who in 1960 announced the end of the Revolution's first phase and the beginning of a new phase, namely industrialisation of the country. Industrialisation meant planning and therefore despotism even over members of the Communist Party. It also meant the predominance of technical men. This explains perhaps a letter from Che Guevara sent on 1 April 1965. Guevara, the typical revolutionary figure, inspired by the most ardent belief in marxism-leninism and the idea of proletarian dictatorship, a romantic figure moved like all revolutionaries by an irresistible desire for radical change and no longer able to endure the new order established in Cuba and its incipient bureaucracy, wrote thus:

'I feel that I have accomplished that part of my duty which bound me to the Cuban Revolution on its own territory and I take my leave of you, of my comrades, of your people who, today, are also my people . . . I have worked with enough integrity and devotion to consolidate the triumph of the Revolution . . . but other countries in the world lay claim to whatever help my modest efforts can provide . . . the time has come for us to part company . . .'[1]

In China, it certainly seems that the beginning of the second phase of order-based society was quick to come about. From 1949 onwards and the early days of agrarian reform requiring organisers and administrators, the ranks of the Chinese Communist Party had to be opened and increased rapidly. Again, later on in 1956 and 1958, a veritable flood of new members was indispensable for organising 'Communes' and for the first 'Great Leap Forward'. Many of the people who joined the Party were recruited from various economic organisations because of their technical competence, whether real or imagined. They were often good technicians but were, politically speaking, sometimes unscrupulous opportunists giving purely formal adherence to marxist-leninism as interpreted by Mao Tse Tung with a view to furthering their own careers. These new Party members very soon showed a bureaucratic mentality that was considered intolerable; they were accused of being over-fond of giving orders and receiving compliments, of trying to extort from visitors enthusiastic comments that they could quote in reports, of constantly pushing themselves to the fore, and of being basically only interested in power, social rank and honour. Mao accused them of opportunism in 1952, 1957, 1960 and 1961 and it became necessary to try to eliminate bureaucratism within the Party and outside it. But in vain, the revisionist opportunists began, in 1960, to occupy important positions within the Party and from 1962 to 1966, a 'clique' of techno-bureaucrats was formed with marked revisionist tendencies in political opposition to Mao Tse Tung. It seemed that China had moved completely into the second phase of order-based societies and that this second phase was in reality technocratic in the guise of marxist-leninism.

Mao Tse Tung's genius found a solution. The aim was to keep China, objectively, within the first phase of a society composed of 'philosophical' orders of a marxist-leninist kind, to maintain revolutionary fervour and to preserve a new society organised and hierarchically structured according to the degree of faith of its members in Mao Tse Tung's thought.

However, in any society, a part of the population always needs some kind of faith to cling to, something to which they give themselves body and soul, enthusiastically, wholeheartedly, unreservedly, without regret or ulterior motives of financial gain or career prospects. This sector of the community is its youth or, at least, a good proportion of them. Mao Tse Tung's idea was that, with each generation, it was essential that young people imbued with his thought should impose on adults and old people a reshaping of ideas, feelings, emotions, attitudes and social behaviour. They should certainly make use of the experience of their elders who should be consulted and utilised by virtue of their expertise, but the young would provide the political momentum behind society and the state, fired as they were with the spirit of revolution in all its intensity and purity. This was the aim of the 'Cultural Revolution' in 1966. Through their young people, every factory, commune and institution became a school for spreading Mao Tse Tung's thought. The whole country, indeed, was one great school teaching Mao's thought. In 1964 Mao laid down that every successive generation should ask for and obtain for itself a renewal of revolutionary zeal. In 1966 he set up the young people, the successors of the Revolution, in opposition to all hierarchies even within the Party. All civil servants were subject to election and could be dismissed. Above all, it was essential that the young should revolt. On 13 June 1966 the examination system set up under the Tang Dynasty was abolished. Universities were closed for one year and lecturers were all screened carefully. Secondary school pupils had to pass a year or two among workers, peasants and soldiers in factories, on communes and in the army, in order to educate themselves in the three revolutionary movements: the class struggle; the struggle for production; the scientific experience. The ones who distinguished themselves by their revolutionary ideology and their militant learnings, their 'strong proletarian attitude' and their 'ability to be as one with the people' could be chosen to study at university, could be 'red and expert'. However, these young students, powerless on their own, had to know how to approach the masses, glean their ideas from them, refine and discuss them, and thereby spark off the spontaneous creativity of the masses, who would, thereafter, move forward of their own accord. With each generation, young people should begin once more to revolt and purify those who went before them until a communist society comes into being.

Since 1965 China had led the world's revolutionary movement which had, in her view, been betrayed by the USSR. Mao's thought, propagated through countless translations of his works, and also perhaps by his emissaries and agents, soon began to rouse a proportion of young students in almost every university in the world. The 'May 1968 Revolution' in France, was just one episode in this world-wide movement. In fact, everywhere there was a growing, secret fear of techno-bureaucratic despotism and the tyranny of the 'Plan', such as to stifle all spontaneity and initiative and even paralyse scientific research that vitally depends on freedom of activity. It created a favourable situation for all kinds of opposition to bureaucracy, and of revolt against technocracy.

Within this diversity of movements, one idea common to all left-wing marxist-leninists became clear, namely that of autonomy of management, of the direct administration of the affairs of city and nation by producers and citizens who themselves make decisions on matters affecting them in workers', peasants' and students' assemblies. They alone were to elect administrators, engineers and teachers chosen according to political criteria, namely whether they were themselves marxist-leninists or at least sympathisers, and these were subject to dismissal at any time if those who elected them chose to do so. Objectively speaking, it was a question

13

of setting up or restoring, according to the country concerned, a 'philosophical' society of orders of a marxist-leninist type, by establishing it as such or by leading it back to the first phase of order-based societies. This is achieved through the revolt of the young, society's leaders in political matters, thereby ensuring that each generation has ideological superiority over its predecessors.

One may ask whether this kind of society would be freer or more spontaneous than a technocratic one. There is reason to doubt whether this is so, bearing in mind the obligation on people to show themselves as ardent marxist-leninists in order to hold responsible positions, to adhere to marxist-leninist ideology purely in order to subsist. Theoretically, the aim is to create a socialist, classless, egalitarian, democratic society. In practice, however, the criterion of marxism-leninist fervour, and the fact that marxism-leninism is imposed on the population if needs be by manipulating assemblies (one technique employed) or by violence, would reduce society to hierarchically arranged orders. On the other hand, the political criterion involved in recruiting technicians, civil servants, engineers and teachers, at the cost of competence in these functions would naturally slow down the process of industrialisation of a country and its progress towards abundance, the condition of true communism. Mao Tse Tung was well aware of this. He puts ideological purity before material results. He is not frightened by the prospect of 1,000 years needed to establish communism. In other words, he envisages the failure of rapid industrialisation for the whole of China. In a country as vast and as populous as China, this is not, moreover, incompatible with the industrialisation of a few select regions and with the making of missiles and the atomic bomb.

It seems therefore that in proportion to their desire for intense industrialisation, in the interests of a rising standard of living and of military power, societies on the way to industrialisation and industrial societies are moving throughout the world towards the form of societies of orders and of estates. But which will triumph in the world? The technocratic society of orders, blueprinted, graded, concerned with elites, having the cult of personality and of the great man, authoritarian and disciplined, totalitarian in tendency, a society which may adopt the marxist-leninist ideology, but may also reject it, for industrialisation, blue-printing and technocracy are interlinked but may exist without marxism-leninism? Or the society of direct, egalitarian and democratic workers' management, but which seems unable to remain so except by rejecting marxist-leninist planning, rapid industrialisation, a substantial rise in living standards, and an age of plenty? It is for men to decide. History has no direction of its own accord, for it is shaped by the will of men and the choices they make. Yet, with every second that passes, men are making their choice by their behaviour.

Note to Conclusion

1. Quoted by Fidel Castro in a speech made on 3 October 1965, *Speech on the Revolution*. Cf. Fidel Castro, *Major Speeches*, 21 Theobald's Road, London W.C.1, 1968, pp. 18–19.

Bibliography

We confine ourselves to indicating certain works, most of which themselves provide a bibliography:

INTRODUCTION

1. Maurice Duverger, *Introduction to the social sciences. With special reference to their methods.* George Allen and Unwin, London, 1964. Praeger Publishers, New York, 1964.
2. Bernard Barber, *Social Stratification.* Harcourt Brace, New York, 1957.

PART I

3. Roland Mousnier, Jean-Pierre Labatut, Yves Durand, *Problèmes de Stratification sociale. Deux cahiers de la noblesse pour les états généraux de la Fronde (1649–1651).* Publications of the Faculté des Lettres et Sciences humaines of Paris–Sorbonne, series 'Textes et Documents', vol. IX, Studies of the Centre de Recherches sur la Civilisation de l'Europe moderne, fasc. 3, Presses Universitaires de France, Paris, 1965.
4. *Problèmes de stratification sociale.* Actes du Colloque international (1966) edited by Roland Mousnier, Publications of the Faculté des Lettres et Sciences humaines of Paris-Sorbonne, series 'Recherches', vol. 43, Studies of the Centre de Recherches sur la Civilisation de l'Europe moderne, fasc. 5, Presses Universitaires de France, Paris, 1968.

PART II

5. Roland Mousnier, *La vénalité des offices sous Henri IV et Louis XIII.* Maugard, Rouen, 1945.

6. *Lettres et mémoires adressés au chancelier Séguier (1633–1649)*. Collected and edited by Roland Mousnier, Publications of the Faculté des Lettres et Sciences humaines of Paris–Sorbonne, series 'Textes et Documents', vols. VI and VII, Studies of the Centre de Recherches sur la Civilisation de l'Europe moderne, (fasc. 2, 1 and 2), Presses Universitaires de France, Paris, 1964.

7. Roland Mousnier, *Peasant Uprisings in Seventeenth-Century France, Russia and China*. George Allen and Unwin, London, 1971. Harper and Row, New York, 1971.

8. Pedro Carrasco, *Land and Polity in Tibet*. University of Washington Press, Seattle, 1959.

9. H. Taine, *The Revolution*. Vol. III, Daldy, Isbister and Co., London, 1878.

10. Albert Soboul, *Précis d'histoire de la Révolution francaise*. Editions Sociales, Paris, 1962.

11. Albert Soboul, *The Parisian Sans-Culottes and the French Revolution, 1793–4*. Clarendon Press, Oxford, 1964. Oxford University Press, New York, 1964.

12. Benito Mussolini, *Fascism. Doctrine and Institutions* [Containing translations of 'La Dottrina del Fascismo', of addresses to the National Corporative Council, 14th Nov. 1933, and in the Senate on the Bill establishing the Corporations, 13th January 1934, and of the Fundamental Laws of Fascism], Ardita, Rome, 1935. (British Museum, 08008.d.10.)

13. C.M.R., *Histoire du fascisme italien*. Paris, 1938.

14. Max Gallo, *L'Italie de Mussolini*. Paris, 1964.

15. Adolf Hitler, *Mein Kampf*. Unexpurgated Edition, Hurst and Blackett, London, 1939.

16. Albert Rivaud, *Le Relèvement de l'Allemagne, (1918–1938)*, 3rd edition, Armand Colin, Paris, 1939.

17. R. D'Harcourt, *L'Evangile de la force*. Plon, Paris, 1936.

18. J. C. Fest, *The Face of the Third Reich*, Weidenfeld and

Nicolson, London, 1970. Pantheon Books, New York, 1970.

19. W. S. Allen, *The Nazi Seizure of Power*. The experience of a single German town 1930–1935, Quadrangle Books, Chicago, 1965.

20. *History of the Communist Party of the Soviet Union (Bolsheviks)*, International Publishers, New York, 1939.

21. Leo Trotsky, *The Revolution betrayed*. Faber and Faber, London, and Doubleday Doran and Co., New York, 1937.

22. David J. Dallin, *The Real Soviet Russia*. Hollis and Carter, London, 1947.

23. Wolfgang Leonhard, *L'Union soviétique*. Editions du Fuseau, Paris, 1953.

24. Bernard Féron, *Où va l'U.R.S.S.*. Editions Temoignage Chretien, Paris, 1958.

25. N. Rutych, *Le Parti communiste au pouvoir*. La Table Ronde, Paris, 1961.

26. Michel Garder, *L'Agonie du régime en Russie soviétique*. La Table Ronde, Paris, 1965.

27. James Burnham, *The Managerial Revolution*. The John Day Co. Inc., New York, 1941.

28. Georges Gurvitch, *Industrialisation et technocratie*. Reports presented at the Première semaine sociologique, Paris, by M. Bayé *et al.*, Armand Colin, Paris, 1948.

29. Jacques Billy, *Les techniciens et le pouvoir*. Presses Universitaires de France, coll. 'Que sais-je?', 881, Paris, 1960.

30. Philippe Bauchard, *Les technocrates et le pouvoir*. Arthaud Paris, 1966.

31. Fidel Castro, *Les étapes de la Révolution cubaine* coll. 'Les Cahiers Libres', no . 61–2, Francois Maspéro, Paris, 1964.

32. Victor Franco, *The Morning After*. A French journalist's impressions of Cuba under Castro, Pall Mall Press, London, 1964. Praeger Publishers, New York, 1963.

33. *Mao Tsê-Tung's quotations; the Red Guard's Handbook.* International Centre, George Peabody's College for Teachers, Nashville, 1967.

34. Han Suyin, *China in the Year 2001.* C. A. Watts and Co., London, 1967. Basic Books, New York, 1967.

Index